9-14-06
22.50

CHÉ

CHE

Original title: *Che, sueño rebelde*
Researched and compiled by: Fernando Diego García, Óscar Sola

Project director: Fernando D. García
Narrative text: Matilde Sánchez
Typography and design: Frank Sozzani

English version: Richard Whitecross, Troth Wells

© **1997 by F.D. García, Ó. Sola**
© **This edition 2000 by New Internationalist Publications Ltd**
   55 Rectory Road, Oxford OX4 1BW, United Kingdom

Published by Pluto Press, 345 Archway Road, London N6 5AA
and 22883 Quicksilver Drive, Sterling, VA 20166-2012, USA

www.plutobooks.com

Printed in the European Union by TJ International, Padstow, England.

10 09 08 07 06 05 04 03 02 01
10 9 8 7 6 5 4 3 2

British Library Cataloguing-in-Publication Data.
A catalogue record for this book is available from the British Library

Library of Congress Cataloging in Publication Data.
Data applied for

ISBN 0-7453-1700-6

CHÉ

IMAGES OF A
REVOLUTIONARY

Compiled by:

FERNANDO DIEGO GARCÍA

ÓSCAR SOLA

Narrative text by:

MATILDE SÁNCHEZ

English version by:

RICHARD WHITECROSS

TROTH WELLS

 Pluto Press
London • Sterling, VA

Acknowledgments

Although Ernesto Guevara lived more than half his life in Argentina, any history of Che has to begin in Cuba. We were able to work there very freely, and everyone who knew him offered us their most fraternal collaboration. Some of his photographs are held in the nation's historical archives, others belong to his *compañeros*, family and friends. Many belong to photographers who took pictures of him and by those who, like us, were able to follow his convictions, his angry outbursts and his moments of happiness in images taken by other people. For this reason, our first expression of gratitude is addressed to the photographers Albert Díaz Korda, Raúl Corrales, Roberto Salas, José Alberto Figueroa, Liborio Noval and Perfecto Romero.

We would particularly like to mention Ana María Erra for generously giving us access to the Ernesto Guevara Lynch Archive; to Pedro Alvarez Tabío and to Efrén González Rodríguez, of the Council of State's Office of Historical Affairs; to Antonio Nuñez Jiménez of the Foundation for Nature and Mankind; to Lesbia Vent Dumois of *Casa de las Américas*. Also to Manuel Martínez Gómez, of *Revista Bohemia*; to Armando Diéguez Suárez, Iris Menales, and Dixi López of *Ediciones Verde Olivo*; to Rolando Rodríguez, of *Editora Política*; to Manuel Martínez and Rosita Muñiz, of *Prensa Latina* and to *Editorial Capitán San Luís*.

We would also like to thank the following people for their support: Aleida March, for her warmth, even during polemical debates; Adys Cupull and Froilán González, for the laborious research they have carried out and their readiness to share it; Richard Dindo, who gave us access to extremely valuable images of Che in Bolivia, and the biographers Paco I. Taibo II, Jon Lee Anderson and Jorge Casteñeda.

In Havana we cannot fail to mention Alberto Granado, Orlando Borrego, Mariano Rodríguez Herrera, Susana Grane – the Argentine Ambassador – William Gálvez, Ulises Estrada, Lupe Álvarez, Delia Luisa López, Marta Pérez-Roló, Luis Adrián Betancourt and Waldo Cárdenas. The professional help provided by Niurka Barroso, and the friendship of Reina María Rodríguez, were invaluable.

In Bolivia, crucial assistance was provided by the Saucedo family, who gave us access to their own archive, as did Juan Carlos Marañon and the photographer Freddy Alborta. In the United States, we were helped by Marina Gilbert and the plastic artists Leandro Katz and Liliana Porter, and in Germany by Martin Franzbach, Matthias Dannel, Graciela Vázquez and José Manuel Rodríguez.

In Argentina, we would like to express out gratitude to Carmen Córdova, Tristan Bauer, Eduardo Longoni, Hugo Gambini, Rogelio García Lupo, Abel Gilbert, Carlos Barrios Barón, Miguel Angel Quarterolo, Valentina Herraz and Patricia Kolesnicov.

The publishers owe a special acknowledgement, once again, to Fernando García and Helen Munín; also to Óscar Sola, Eliana, Lea and Angelika Bussas, who now appreciate everything that is hidden behind these acknowledgements.

CONTENTS

CHÉ

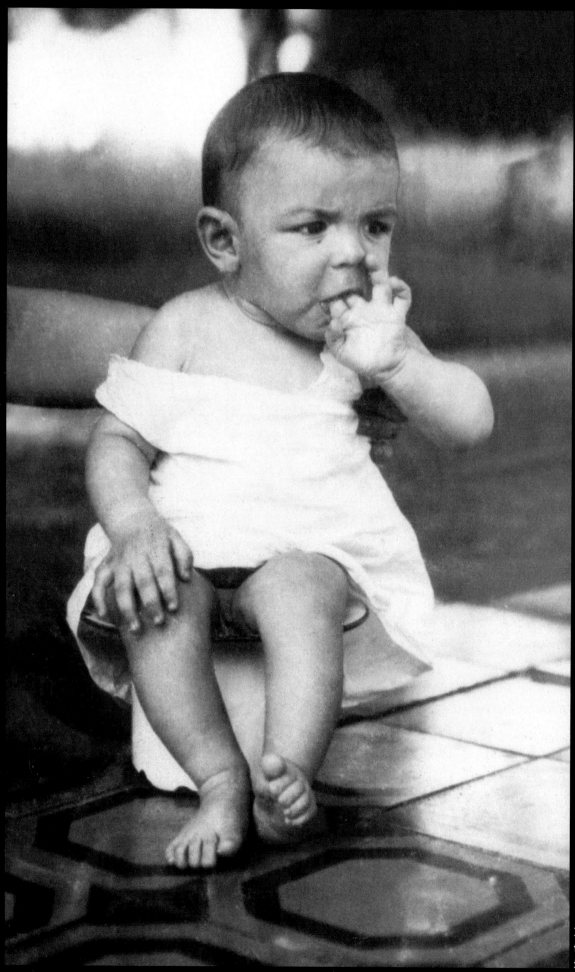

Even heroes have
to undergo
initiation rites.

THE HERO AS A CHILD

E rnesto 'Che' Guevara was descended from adventurers of every kind, who had founded distinguished families. He lived in a vast, sparsely populated country – Argentina – that was peopled by a range of imported identities. The boy grew up thinking of the whole world as his family, and so was unlikely to stay in the land where he happened to have been born. Such were the origins of the child destined to become a hero.

1928

Night had fallen on 14th June as the prospective parents were traveling along the Paraná, an Argentinian river five times longer than the island of Cuba. The passenger boat on its way to Buenos Aires made a stop at the city of Rosario. The couple left the boat since the woman – Celia de la Serna de Guevara – was going into labor. She reached the hospital in time to give birth to her first child, who was named after his father. Shortly after he was born, the child contracted pulmonary congestion, an unfortunate inheritance from his forebears. Jon Lee Anderson's biography repeats an old family rumor which suggested that Celia was already pregnant when she married – a rumor indirectly confirmed by the long-standing family debate as to whether Ernesto was born prematurely, or at term.

It used to be said, with the ironic humor so characteristic of the country, that all you had to do to become an aristocrat in Argentina was to stake your claim to a piece of land ahead of anyone else. As members of a rural aristocracy founded, no doubt, by some pioneering cattle rancher, Ernesto's father and mother were both

Rosario, 1928. The first child of a bohemian couple.

★

Ernesto Guevara Lynch, more ancestry than money.

Celia de la Serna, a young, bold, atheistic modern woman.

Che's North American grandfather, a geographer and explorer.

considered to have come from 'better' families. The cosmopolitan origins of the country gradually shaped a unique national identity and produced a culture which thanks to a New World tendency to carry imitation to excess was even more liberal and universalist than that of Europe.

The two bloodlines that came together in the young Ernesto's father, don Ernesto Guevara Lynch, could be traced back more than ten generations. In this vast new southern land, such a heritage ensured that the family would have a place in the ranks of the founding fathers. One of his great-great-grandfathers had been Viceroy of New Spain (Mexico), and his son had eloped with his bride from Louisiana. The Guevaras came to the River Plate in the middle of the 18th century, but 100 years later gold fever attracted them to California. As a result, in spite of his distinguished Argentinian roots, Ernesto's grandfather Roberto had been born a US citizen. Towards the end of the 19th century he married Ana María Lynch, a woman of Irish descent whose family had settled in Argentina 40 years earlier. Grandfather Roberto had been a founder of that bastion of the great Argentinian landowners, the *Sociedad Rural Argentina*. The son of a fortune-hunter and landowner, he was a geographer and carried out a survey of the Argentinian Chaco, the vast wilderness extending across the northern frontier of south-east Bolivia. His evocative tales of those times, full of the resinous scents and sounds of the whispering trees, would lull the child to sleep. The young

Ernesto grew up with a special affection for Roberto's wife, who was known as Grandmother Ana.

Celia de la Serna's family had a less adventurous past, but was closer to political power. One of her ancestors, General José de la Serna e Hinojosa, had been the last Viceroy of colonial Peru. Her father, Juan Martín, had been politically active in the early days of the Radical Civic Union (UCR), the first political party in Argentina to attract significant support, soon after it came into being in the 1890 Revolution. In 1928, the year Ernesto was born, the long-standing leader of the Party, Hipólito Yrigoyen, had just begun his second term as President. It would appear that Celia, an educated woman, felt deeply uncomfortable with the predictable life that women of her class and at that time were expected to follow. She was also special in having been orphaned and subsequently brought up by her older sister, Carmen de la Serna, who in 1928 married the communist intellectual Cayetano Córdova Iturburu.

In spite of her parochial education at the Sacred Heart school in Buenos Aires, Celia always considered herself a 'modern' woman, which she proved to her anxious family by bobbing her hair and driving a car. Even more worrying for them was her decision to marry Ernesto Guevara Lynch, a student who failed to complete his architecture degree, a cultured young

In a family of adventurers, this great-grandfather searched for gold in California.

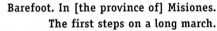

Barefoot. In [the province of] Misiones. The first steps on a long march.

MAMÁ USED TO SIT US ON THE HORSE THEN LET GO, TO SEE WHAT WOULD HAPPEN. PAPÁ INSISTED THAT WE SHOULDN'T USE STIRRUPS, BECAUSE HE WAS AFRAID WE'D BE CAUGHT UP IN THEM. SO WE LEARNT TO RIDE WITHOUT. WE ALWAYS PLAYED GAMES AND MADE UP THE RULES. THERE WAS LOTS OF SPACE. IN THE COUNTRY.

Ana María Guevara

Alta Gracia, 1933. A postcard that foretells the future: donkeys, mules, and horses. Che could breathe more freely when he was riding.

The dismounted rider, hat in hand, already knows when to ask "Daddy, my injection".

man with entrepreneurial drive on whom fortune never smiled. In 1967, he wrote, 'I may not have made a great fortune, but no one can say I have been a ne'er-do-well, or that I haven't tried to put together all kinds of businesses, and always tried out new ideas.' The couple's lives were marked by the broad gap between their privileged backgrounds and their limited financial resources. The only land they owned was Celia's, and that had to be rented out. They both belonged to a particular social class – the down-at-heel aristocracy.

Celia had an Andalucian air that was accentuated by the black hair she wore clipped short. In pictures, she always looks as if she expected to have a better future. As he grew older, her son inherited the rather severe look which gave her an air of superiority. Ernesto senior, on the other hand, passed on his softer traits: the short, straight nose, and his eyes with their melancholy expression.

The Guevara de la Sernas lived in the town of Caraguatay, in the north-eastern province of Misiones, where her father had a *yerba maté* (herbal tea) plantation that never quite managed to make a profit. From that time, there would always be a place for *maté* in Ernesto's life. By the end of 1929, Celia had given birth to her second child, a daughter who was named after her. She worked off the tension between her housewifely duties and her progressive views by making spectacular dives into the river. Just before Ernesto's second birthday, Celia took him into the water with her, and he developed acute pneumonia. This was the beginning of the illness – asthma – that would lead to the family moving and have a fundamental effect on Ernesto's life. It was one of the keys to his identity, providing the basis of his extraordinary willpower and acting as the anvil on which his character was forged.

There is always a barrier on the road to becoming a hero, and Ernesto's whole life, and even his death, can be seen as a *tour de force* against his illness. Some time after becoming a revolutionary he wrote to his mother saying that 'I depend more on my inhaler than on my rifle'. In the circumstances, there is a certain reckless breathlessness in the pipes, cigars and cigarettes that he smoked in the Sierra Maestra campaign in Cuba and later on, in the absurdly over-sized cigars that as Industry Minister he handed out for propaganda purposes and as a token of the Cuban Revolution. There is a certain breathlessness too in his wanderlust.

In 1932, the Guevara de la Sernas family moved to a house in San Isidro, an elegant district in the northern suburbs of Buenos Aires, but its proximity to the river proved bad for the sickly boy. A year later, they moved further inland to the province of Córdoba, which has a drier climate, and settled in

THE SICKNESS MAY EVEN HAVE MADE HIM STRONGER, BY TEACHING HIM HOW TO CONTROL HIMSELF, AND NOT TO BE CARRIED AWAY BY HIS EMOTIONS OR PERSUADED BY OTHER PEOPLE. I SUPPOSE THAT, GENERALLY SPEAKING, THE SUFFERING PRODUCED BY ASTHMA EVENTUALLY CREATES ITS OWN SELF-DEFENSE MECHANISMS.

Ernesto Guevara Lynch

Ernesto and his sister, Celia; a relationship of passionate competition.

> CHAOS REIGNED, AND THEY ONLY MADE A SERIOUS ATTEMPT TO CLEAN UP WHEN THERE WAS SOMETHING TO CELEBRATE. MY SISTER CELIA, WHO WAS VERY SLOPPY, HAD ADJUSTED TO HER HUSBAND'S CAREFREE WAY OF LIFE. BUT THEY ALL SEEMED TO BE HAPPY IN THAT "LIVE AND LET LIVE" ATMOSPHERE.
>
> *Carmen de la Serna*

Celia with her children. Against medical advice, she encouraged Ernesto to live an outdoor life.

Alta Gracia, a hill town with the charm of a summer resort. By this time, although Guevara Lynch had become a builder, the family was still largely supported by Celia's own meagre income.

One of Córdoba's attractions at the time was its mules. Tourists used to like being photographed on them, and took back souvenirs with mule motifs. Ernesto learnt the pleasures of riding in Córdoba where he lived until he was 17. He also imagined himself in a traditional Argentinian role – that of the national hero, San Martín, who in 1817 depended on mules when he crossed the Andes to liberate Chile. Mules and horses continued to have significance in Guevara's life, as best means of crossing difficult terrain.

Che's asthma attacks in childhood meant that to begin with he led a rather sheltered life. Since he was not well enough to go to school, he was taught to read and write by his mother. She awakened his voracious hunger for reading. According to Celia, while he regularly attended the second and third grades of primary school, he had to get through the next three years as best he could, only attending class when he felt well enough to do so. His brothers and sisters brought back work for him from school, but he was eight years old before he could attend on a regular basis. Biographers and witnesses agree that Celia had an enormous influence on her son's intellectual ambitions. Her example drove Ernesto to be successful for her sake, and even to exceed her maternal hopes. He wanted to surpass her dreams for him, and knew that wherever he was she would be following his life in the newspapers. In due course, Celia became radicalized in the same way as her son, and found her own path to liberation, recalling the contribution she had made to the destiny of this new liberator of the Americas. Her son's love for her was torn between his refusal to be overprotected and his drive to fulfil the dreams his mother had instilled in him. His passionate commitment was matched by Celia de la Serna's gradual radicalization during the 1960s; mother and the son were growing up together.

Biographers have often played down the influence of Che's father, but it was Ernesto senior who molded his son's mind and trained his body. During the long days of convalescence he taught Ernesto a love of chess. He also took care of him when his wife was occupied with their other children. Che's father gave him the adrenaline injections he needed to dilate his bronchial passages, and connected his mask to the oxygen tube. He also contributed to Che's determination to overcome his illness by insisting that he learn to swim, believing that he must never give in to his physical difficulties. His father also introduced him to shooting, so that by the

Ernesto, Celia, Ana María and Roberto in the swimming pool with their mother and father.

time he was five 'Ernestito' knew what to do. We can imagine the adult's hand guiding his aim, holding his tiny hands; the hands of father and son joined together on the same weapon.

The first letter from a prolific writer: "Dear Auntie Beatriz..."

The family album

The oldest child is in the center, surrounded by the younger children: Celia, Roberto, Ana María, and – in pictures taken some years later – Juan Martín. In the photos Ernesto is almost invariably smiling. Perhaps he felt obliged to be as cheerful as his siblings, and not to disappoint the camera. In *Ernesto Guevara, también conocido como el Che* ('Ernesto Guevara, also known as Che') a biography full of insights, the novelist Paco Taibo II looks with pity on the asthmatic child, stepping partly-clothed into the waters where other holidaymakers are frolicking and enjoying themselves. At the public swimming-pool, he knew when it wasn't safe for him to go into the water. There was a sense in which his physical limitations broadened his inner world, and gave him the determination of an adult. He looks angry because he didn't want to be included in the photo, and he stands out precisely because his clothes make it clear that he's not fully well. This training in stoicism is already introducing him to the pleasures of privation. So he does, in other respects, have a normal childhood.

A CROSS BETWEEN JACK LONDON AND BAUDELAIRE

Salgari's story of Sandokán the pirate, one of Che's childhood heroes.

Ana María, encouraging her brother.

Ernesto's irregular school attendance fitted in well with growing up on the streets and living a free and varied life. There were plenty of formal parties to bring the family together dressed in their finest clothes, but in the back rooms of the various Guevara houses in the hills of Córdoba – one of them a family hotel – the air was free from prejudice, and different social classes mixed easily.

Young Ernesto grew up out of doors, in the meritocracy of the local boys' gangs. In that society, stoicism and physical endurance were ideal gifts, and gave Ernesto a sense of moral leadership. When out with the other boys he learnt that bravery is most effective when it is cloaked in modesty. By the time he was ten, he also knew how to give himself adrenaline injections.

Ernesto was one of those boys who read a lot. Having started with poetry, in his teens he devoured the classical children's library from Jules Verne and Jack London to the Argentinian author, Horacio Quiroga. Everything he did involved a compromise between movement and physical restriction. Since his body was not strong enough to exhaust his childish

The family pastime: reading.

energy, he applied it to reading or playing chess. Novels gave a structure to his need for action, and a geographical basis – lands to discover – to his urge to understand more of the world. As well as adventures, he read *risqué* poets in the French his mother had taught him. He was especially interested in the works of Charles Baudelaire, whose poems about travel as a mystical experience made a deep impression on him. Baudelaire, the poet of the night, provided an early link from French poetry to North American road novels. French, at that time still the language of the Argentinian cultural élite, helped to shape Ernesto Guevara's intellectual elegance and sense of style.

A scruffy caddy. Childhood in Córdoba, in a society of equals.

THE WAY WE WERE BROUGHT UP WAS TOTALLY ANTI-CHURCH. IN SUMMER WE USED TO HAVE GAMES OF FOOTBALL WHERE THE ONES WHO BELIEVED IN GOD PLAYED THOSE OF US WHO DIDN'T. THERE WERE ONLY FOUR OR FIVE OF US. ALL THE OTHER KIDS IN OUR GANG WERE BELIEVERS. THE ONLY ONES WHO'D PLAY ON OUR SIDE WERE THE TWO VIROSA BOYS, WHO WERE THE SONS OF SPANISH REPUBLICANS. THE CATHOLICS USED TO SCORE MASSES OF GOALS, AND THEY USED TO FEEL BETTER WHEN THEY BEAT THE UNBELIEVERS.

Roberto Guevara

Ernesto and Roberto, partners in adventure.

Córdova Ituburu, Che's communist uncle, who was a newspaper correspondent in the Spanish Civil War.

1937

Seven years earlier, President Hipólito Yrigoyen had been overthrown in Argentina's first *golpe* or coup. The country was in the middle of what became known as 'the decade of infamy', a period marked by electoral fraud and by government policies that were effectively determined by the cattle-raising élite. Due to the large number of Spanish immigrants in Argentina, any news of the Spanish Civil War was followed with intense interest. Reports from the front fanned debate among the middle class. The Civil War was re-enacted in central Buenos Aires, which was crowded with Spaniards, many of them political exiles; every day new barricades sprung up on both sides of the Avenida de Mayo, the main street. In Córdoba, Ernesto and his best friends played 'Republicans and *Franquistas*', a variation on the Cowboys and Indians theme. Thanks to the Rodríguez Aguilars, a family in exile from Spain, and his uncle Cayetano Córdova Iturburu, a war correspondent for the newspaper *Crítica*, Ernesto had access to eyewitness accounts and pictures. By the time he was ten he was reading Republican authors such as Federico García Lorca and Antonio Machado, hardly suspecting that one day he would meet León Felipe in Central America, and share a destiny similar to that of the Republicans. The boy who became Che Guevara could have been seen as the last recruit to the International Brigades, and his death as romantic as that of any Republican anti-hero.

In the 1940s, Argentina was one of the world's richest nations, and the intellectual beacon of Latin America. Most boys whose parents could afford the fees chose the private Montserrat high school, but the family opted for the more liberal Dean Funes in the provincial capital, which meant Ernesto would have to travel over 20 miles each day.

It was in the city of Córdoba – traditionally known as *Córdoba la docta* because of its status as Argentina's oldest university – that Ernesto made very close friendships which lasted for the rest of his life. They included the Ferrer brothers, Jorge and Carlos (nicknamed 'Calica'), and Gustavo Roca, the son of

Photographs sent by Uncle Córdova. Ernesto used to mark the Republicans' victories and defeats on a map.

Alta Gracia, 1938.
Dressed in white for
Ana María's birthday.

Deodoro Roca (one of the 1918 Reformers). Gustavo recalls Ernesto's daily visits
to his father's library: 'He was a Reformer in those days, when being a Reformer
meant being left-wing. I think that the Reform had something to do with
Ernesto's ideological development.' However, it has to be said that any number
of people claim they were the first to interest Ernesto in radical politics.

About this time Ernesto met Tomás and Alberto Granado, who
encouraged him to take up what was considered the upper-class sport of
rugby. If any sport should have been off-limits to Ernesto, it was this one.
But thanks to what might be called 'the logic of prohibition' – and despite
his father's insistence that he should stop playing – rugby very quickly
became a violent alternative to convalescing in bed. Running left him
breathless when he was playing, but he also found that it helped to improve
his breathing at other times. He often had to break off his training to use
his inhaler, but overcame his handicap with the sort of outright
dismissiveness that befits an anti-hero. His flamboyant personality inspired
many nicknames. When he was young his family used to call him Ernestito or
Teté, but on the rugby field he rebaptized himself with his battle cry of 'Out
of the way! Here comes Furibundo!' This name (shortened to 'Fuser') meant
'wild', or 'furious'. Ernesto/Fuser played at such a hard pace that because of
his asthma he did not always survive to the end of the match, but there was
usually a friend or relative on the touchline to help him.

The pictures of the family at Mar del Plata show an elegant beach resort

Pampa de Achala, 1937.
A walk in the snow.

Just 16, and Ernesto begins to discover that he has winning ways.

in the finest Côte d'Azur style, with a majestic promenade beside a rough and chilly sea. At the time, every middle-class family had their photograph taken striking exactly the same pose as the Guevara de la Sernas.

In spite of the asthma, Ernesto lived intensively. Always surrounded by friends, he grew up in the brotherhood of athletics and macho locker-room humor. Many described him as being unusually bold. Fernando Barral, a Spanish boy exiled in Córdoba with his mother, recalls 'his complete lack of fear of any danger... he was very confident, and completely independent in his ideas'. Adolescence is the age when ethical convictions are formed, and Ernesto fed on ideas that would only reveal themselves at a later date. He considered that his education would not be complete until he had extended his personal experience by traveling in Latin America. He was of a generation that had begun to think of youth not as a stage on the way to adulthood, but as the supreme moment in one's life. In a sense he never outgrew that stage, since he was constantly rethinking himself, and never felt at home in formal institutions... and because he died such an early death. His vision of youth as an age of glorious privilege also explains the impact he had on the youth of the 1960s. Ernesto was a visionary, someone who captured the spirit of his age ahead of time.

Building character

It was during this time that Ernesto won his least metaphorical nickname – pig – which related to his ability to spend a week without changing clothes.

Mar del Plata: by this time Juan Martín had joined the family.

Inseparable friends. The three players standing in line next to Ernesto are the Granado brothers.

His only shirt was dubbed 'the week-longer'. Even today in Buenos Aires, whenever a relative shows up looking especially unkempt, his family says 'you look like a Guevara'. Ernesto's prominent forehead led to a second nickname: *pitecantropus rectus* (ape-man). His father disclosed that because Ernesto's allergies to certain foods set off respiratory crises, his son made up for enforced fasting with serious bingeing. In his controversial book, *Mi amigo el Che* ('My Friend Che') Ricardo Rojo says that 'he ate ravenously, in vast quantities, taking as much time as he could, and enjoying himself with unconcealed delight. Later on he went through a more ascetic period.' Ernesto himself used to explain that he was eating 'to build up a reserve'.

The country was living through events that would determine its political course for the rest of the century. After the nationalist *golpe* (coup) of 1943, the rising head of the Labor Secretariat, Colonel Juan Domingo Perón, polarized public opinion. The unprecedented involvement in politics by unionized urban workers and more marginal groups was resented by the middle classes, and like most professionals and intellectuals, the Guevara de la Sernas were opposed to Peronism. While the population was split sharply between devotion and loathing, it seems that Ernesto had not reached any firm view. On the contrary, the only conflicts that appealed to him as worthy causes involved foreign countries. During the Second World War, after Ernesto's father had joined an anti-fascist group called *Acción Argentina*, Ernesto went along, obtained his own membership card, and took an interest in tracking the contacts between some of the people who spoke on behalf of the German cause, and the sizeable (pro-Nazi) German community in the Córdoba hills.

In the debate about Guevara's indifference to Peronism, some writers have noted that he must have been suspicious about the populist approach

THE VAST WARDROBES OF THOSE TIMES PROVIDED A PERFECT HIDING PLACE FOR CERTAIN FORBIDDEN EXPERIENCES. IN HIS EARLY ADOLESCENCE, THIS WAS THE HIDING PLACE ERNESTO CHOSE TO OVERCOME HIS EMBARRASSMENT, AND WHERE HE ASKED HIS COUSIN CARMEN: "TELL ME, HAVE YOU HAD YOURS YET?"

Carmen Córdova, 'La Negrita'. His first love.

Juan Martín ('Patatín')
A younger brother to Ernesto.

TWO FRIENDS RAN FOR SHELTER

UNDER A TREE. THEY WERE

FLEEING A THUNDER CLAP THAT

TOOK THEM BY SURPRISE.

BOOM... THE THUNDER CAME

CRASHING DOWN. BUT THE ONE

WITH THE IMAGE OF SAN

CRISPINITO... THAT ONE...

HE WAS THE ONE WHO DIED.

A heretical verse that Ernesto used to recite to Juan Martín.

of the movement. On the other hand, to have signed up with the opposition would have put him alongside his parents, with the reactionaries, and with the US Ambassador, Spruille Braden. Anderson observes that the Peronist slogans about political sovereignty and economic independence must have held some attraction for Ernesto, given the parallels with *The Discovery of India* by the Indian leader, Nehru, which he read at the time. However, up to the time when Perón was overthrown in 1955, there is nothing to suggest that he felt such an attraction.

Ernesto was called up for military service in February 1946, at the same time as the Presidential elections which were won by Juan Perón. He applied for, and was granted, a deferment. The story goes that years later when he was called up a second time, he took a long bath in freezing water just before the medical examination, and so, thanks to an asthma attack, he was discharged. Given this track record it is ironic that from 1955 until his death he was able to lead the life of a soldier, in a career that he began as a guerrilla fighter and ended as a commanding officer.

The 1940s

In the 1940s, an Argentinian was seen as one who had a cultural homeland halfway between the Americas and Europe. For decades, Buenos Aires had seen itself as the bridge between the two continents. As Jorge Luis Borges once joked, a middle-class Argentinian, being essentially a European in exile, was someone who deserved a better break. There was another view, which was that ever since the country won its independence in 1810, Argentinian liberalism also retained a certain Latin Americanist drive, an underlying desire for regional integration. Ernesto, perhaps without realising it, also tried to bring the two Americas together.

By the time Che finished secondary school, family expectations began to weigh heavily on him as the oldest son. He wanted to stay in Córdoba to read Engineering, but when his paternal grandmother, Ana, fell gravely ill he went to look after her in Buenos Aires until her death. While he was taking care of her, he had his first revelation: having been forced to cope with his own illness, he decided to study medicine at the University of Buenos Aires. And in the hope that he might discover a cure for his own allergy, he chose asthma as his area of research.

1947

At this time Guevara Lynch's business drifted into decline. Argentina, now becoming seen as 'the grain basket of the world', began to prosper from the recovery of the European economy after the Second World War. Many urban

"The paradoxical sparkle of those green eyes told me it would be dangerous to fall asleep in them...", in a letter from Ernesto to Chichina Ferreyra, October 20th 1951.

I HEARD THE SQUELCHING SOUND OF HER SHOELESS FEET

IN THE BOAT

AND COULD IMAGINE THOSE NIGHT-TIME SIGNS OF HUNGER.

MY HEART WAS A PENDULUM, SWINGING BETWEEN HER AND

THE ROAD.

WHERE DID I FIND THE STRENGTH TO FREE MYSELF FROM

HER EYES?

I SLIPPED FROM HER ARMS.

SHE STOOD, CLOUDING HER DISTRESS WITH TEARS,

BEYOND THE RAIN AND THE WINDOW.

BUT SHE COULDN'T BRING HERSELF TO CALL AFTER ME:

"WAIT! I'M COMING WITH YOU!"

Ernesto, in a bitter-sweet mood, transcribed these verses by Otera Silva in his Travel Notes, to record Chichina's farewell.

Uncle Jorge de la Serna, who encouraged Ernesto's eccentricities, started him off as an amateur pilot.

NOW I KNOW, ALMOST AS IF IT WERE A MATTER OF FATE, AND I HAD NO CHOICE, THAT MY DESTINY IS TO TRAVEL. OR RATHER, OUR DESTINY, SINCE IN THIS RESPECT ALBERTO THINKS THE SAME AS ME. PERHAPS, SOME DAY, WHEN I'M TIRED OF ROAMING THE WORLD, I'LL SETTLE DOWN AGAIN IN THIS LAND OF ARGENTINA.

Ernesto Guevara. Travel Notes, 1952.

THE CALL OF THE ROAD

La Poderosa II, a two-wheeled companion for traveling through Latin America with Alberto Granado.

Uncle and nephew at the El Palomar airfield, 1950.

Temporary jobs, experiences with hospitable girls, dust-ups in small-town dance-halls... the friends were traveling through time, as if they were adrift in space. The 'dynamic duo' took two months to reach Santiago de Chile, where *La Poderosa II* gave up on them. So they continued on foot; the riders turned into tramps. Ernesto wrote with remarkable irony about their 'descent to a lower class', on what was in fact becoming a journey into a state of poverty, which they jokingly described as 'a gift of the road'. This transition marked the beginning of the 'de-Argentinizing' of Ernesto Guevara.

When the friends reached the vast Antofagasta copper mines in northern Chile, Ernesto noted that 'The vast scale of the mine can be accounted for by the 10,000 corpses in the cemetery.' The spectacle of the miners spoke a truth to him about Latin America's evolution, and how the splendor of its mythical past contrasted with present-day misery. Along the way, Ernesto recited from the works of the Chilean poet, Pablo Neruda, and from José Martí, the father of Cuban independence. As a poet and a lawyer, an ideologist of the new State, and a man of action who sacrificed himself for his ideas, Martí is crucial to our understanding of the man Ernesto was to become.

From Antofagasta they continued north to Peru, the cradle of mythical South America. Having been brought up in a country largely populated by immigrants, and with a very limited pre-Conquest history, Ernesto quickly developed a passion for Peru's indigenous culture. There are certain recurring patterns in this story. To begin with, Ernesto traveled to escape from having nothing to do, and preferred to learn independently – far from home, and without the help of educational institutions. His ability to switch from the university to

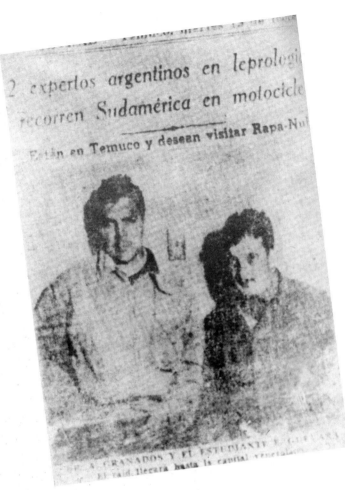

A Chilean newspaper, the *Austral*, published in Temuco, welcomes the friends as "two Argentine experts in the field of leprosy".

In Santiago de Chile, *La Poderosa II* gives up on them. Now they have become "hobos with no means of transport".

Santiago de Chile, March 1952. Even the faces of the people reminded him of Córdoba.

the open road was also remarkable. When he was traveling he felt that everything was worthwhile, because everything left an impression, and there was no wasted time. Traveling in effect becomes a pilgrimage, not just in the sense of a *via crucis* (stations of the cross) where every station represents one more shrine to poverty; but even more than that: a path leading to self-knowledge through action. Ernesto had read Freud, and knew the basic theories of modern psychoanalysis. He also recognized that he was traveling in order to know himself. It just so happened that Ernesto's metaphysical search demanded of him that he should also change the world – and that the revelations and revolutions he experienced in his life would take place far from home.

Ernesto was notorious for wanting to reach the top of the next mountain. This spirit took him to the mouth of the Chilean mines, and the peak of Huayna Picchu, just as he would in due course scale the volcanoes in Mexico and Mount Turquino in Cuba. He climbed to find clear air, and to see the full picture. However, the ascent did not prevent him from carrying out a reconnaissance of the land. In his last Bolivian diary he recorded the details of the terrain – following the example of his grandfather, Roberto Guevara, who had explored the Argentinian Chaco – but he did so more in the style of an explorer than as a guerrilla fighter.

In the first week of April the two friends left the valley of the Urubamba River outside Cuzco, Peru, and set off for the leper colony at Huambo. By this stage, though they had no money left, they took a certain pride in traveling like the poor, taking the view that their disdain for money amounted to a rejection of bourgeois values. At times, it seemed as if the only purpose of their trip was to test the solidarity of the local people. They always found a Good Samaritan, who in this instance took on the guise of a communist leper doctor. In Lima, Dr Hugo Pesce fed them, and gave them two leftover suits. A social worker at the leper colony who had a brief romance with Ernesto received a letter from him that was practically a profession of faith: 'To Zoraida, with the hope that she will always be ready to receive a pair of aimless drifters, on their way from anywhere to anywhere, always down and out, without a past or a future.'

The travelers reached Iquitos, in the Amazon rainforest, and with it a new station of the cross: the San Pablo leper colony. Ernesto overcame the tide and swam across the torrent. The lepers built a log raft

The ruins of Ollantayambo, near Cuzco, April 1952.

YOU HAVE TO BELIEVE IN THE CURRENT THAT

CARRIES THE RAFT MADE BY THE POOR

YOUNG MEN. YOU HAVE TO BELIEVE IN

SOMEONE WHO CAN ONLY TRUST IN THE

BLESSINGS OF THE POOR AT THE START OF A

DANGEROUS JOURNEY. AND YOU HAVE TO

BELIEVE IN THE JOURNEY, IF THE ONLY PEOPLE

TO BID THEM FAREWELL WERE THE SICK

AND WOUNDED ON THE RIVER BANK.

Fina García Marruz. 'Oratorio for Che Guevara'.

With Alberto Granado,
as they leave the San
Pablo leper colony. The
raft eventually ended up
drifting away down the
Amazon River.

The *Mambo-Tango* raft was a present
from the lepers to the young
Argentines. At this point they really
had become "idle drifters". The photo
was taken on Friday, June 20th 1952.

Fishing for *zóngano* fish.

"Your son's missing you, right down to his elbows, his heels and his backside."

for the Argentinians, with a small cabin to protect them from the rain. The *Mambo-Tango* was a raft worthy of the Swiss Family Robinson, a hobo's home-from-home that foreshadowed the journey on the precarious *Granma*. In the photos Ernesto seems to be dressed as a sailor on shore at Carnival time. His striped T-shirt makes him look quite feminine, with the ambiguous masculinity of a Mardi Gras sailor prowling the ports at night.

Colombia, which at that time was under the authoritarian regime of Laureano Gómez, struck them as rather hostile, so they changed course for Venezuela. Ernesto still had to keep the promise he had made to his mother about sitting for his final exams. On July 24th, 1952 he asked his girlfriend, Tita Infante, to enrol him in three courses.

Tita continued to be his favorite correspondent for a number of years. With her, he kept up a typical friendship of never-consummated flirtation. She was Ernesto's female mirror image, and he put on a great narcissistic display, keeping her torch aflame in beautifully-crafted letters whose formality only added to their seductiveness. He invariably addressed Tita as *Usted*, the formal word in Spanish for 'you', and in turn he would never let her call him 'Che'. According to her family, Tita was deeply in love with Ernesto, but although he later invited her several times to practice psychiatry in Cuba, he never proposed. After he was killed she suffered from terrible depression, and wrote him a moving posthumous letter. Towards the end of 1976 – which was perhaps the most tragic year of the century for Argentina following the military coup – she committed suicide.

End of the journey

Ernesto and Alberto parted in Venezuela. Alberto took a job working with lepers, while Ernesto found a seat on a cargo plane that was transporting horses to Argentina via Miami. His by now well-developed anti-imperialist feelings led him to comment that he would 'rather be an illiterate Indian than a North American millionaire'. Back home on Calle Aráoz, he realized when he re-read his notebook that the trip had changed him more than he had imagined. The diary closes with a fictional aside that dramatizes the 'before and after' of his discoveries, and speaks of taking a fond farewell to his homeland. His somewhat obscure prose sets out a number of partly unformed and inconsistent predictions and utopian hopes. The narrator is transformed into another character, a revolutionary exiled from a bourgeois Europe, who presents himself to the author with a fatalistic view of history. The author replies, with a promise that conveys all the pathos of his 24 years: 'I will take the side of the people, and I know, because I can see it written in the night, that I, an eclectic dissector of doctrines, a psychoanalyst of dogmas, screaming like a man possessed, who would attack the barricades and the trenches, and drench my weapons in blood... I am tensing my body, ready for the fight, and preparing my being as a sacred shrine so that it might resound with the new vibrations and hopes of that primordial cry of the triumphant working class/ proletariat.'

At this time, in terms of his university career, Ernesto seemed to be less interested in finishing his studies than in settling a debt with his family. And so another university *tour de force* came about, since in just three months he passed all the exams for 14 courses. For the Guevara de la Sernas, this was the fulfilment of their middle-class urban dream: they had a doctor for a son. But Ernesto's achievement would only serve to confirm his rejection of that world. He prepared to return to 'Latin America with a capital "L"', this time with another childhood friend from Córdoba, Carlos 'Calica' Ferrer. On July 7 th 1953, they boarded a train for Bolivia.

His parents remembered their son at the Retiro station in Buenos Aires. He turned round, crying out euphorically 'A soldier of America is leaving!' The next time they saw him was in 1959 in Havana, as a victorious leader of the Cuban Revolution.

The friends reached La Paz on July 24th. Bolivia held out the prospect of political agitation. In 1952, a coalition of workers' and peasants' militias had overthrown the Army, imposing their own conditions. The government of President-elect Víctor Paz Estenssoro was a shaky coalition that was pushing forward radical measures. When Ernesto arrived, it had just introduced a far-ranging program of land reform for which the continent had no precedent. The situation was tense, and there were predictions of a civil war.

In La Paz, the two friends met Ricardo Rojo, an Argentinian lawyer who represented political prisoners and was opposed to the Peronist government. Rojo recalls that 'Ernesto didn't say much. He preferred to listen to the others, until suddenly, with a reassuring smile, he would let fly with some crushing remark.'

The travelers continued to head northwards. After a brief stop in Peru to climb Machu Picchu Ernesto wrote in his diary: 'Citizens of South America: now is the time to reclaim the past.' They then moved on to Guayaquil in

Tita Infante, fellow student and confidante.

I WOULD REALLY LIKE TO INJECT YOU WITH SOME OF THAT HIGHLY MATERIALISTIC LOVE I HAVE FOR LIFE, WHICH I AM CONSCIOUS OF ENJOYING EVERY MOMENT OF THE DAY.

Letter from Ernesto.

WE WERE JOINED IN A VERY CLOSE INTIMACY, WHICH MEANT WE COULD CONFIDE IN EACH OTHER ABOUT ANYTHING HAPPY OR SAD THAT HAPPENED TO US. AT THE SAME TIME, BECAUSE OF HIS CHARACTERISTIC RESERVE ABOUT INTIMATE MATTERS, WE WERE ABLE TO COMMUNICATE SO MUCH TO EACH OTHER IN JUST A FEW WORDS.

Tita Infante, Evocación.

Ecuador, where their poverty became destitution; Ernesto survived by eating nothing but bananas. Their time in Guayaquil involved spending whole days in limbo. They had no money, but the last thing they wanted to do was to go home. Ernesto could only dream of the future, which included the need to earn enough money to pay for his ailing mother's treatment in Paris. Indecision about what he should do next wore him down, and made him vulnerable to other people's bright ideas. That was how another Argentinian in the group, Eduardo 'Gualo' García, was able to launch a proposal for traveling on to Guatemala so that they could 'see something new – a left-wing revolution'. They managed to get free passages on different steamships heading for Central America. During a brief stay in San José, Costa Rica, Ernesto met two future presidents: the Venezuelan, Rómulo Betancourt, who struck him as a luke-warm reformer, and the Dominican writer, Juan Bosch. In the Soda Palace Bar in San José he came into contact for the first time with Cuban revolutionaries. A pair of exiles told of the assault on the Moncada Barracks on July 26th that year and they praised a brilliant Cuban lawyer from a good family who had just managed to extract his freedom from the dictator, Fulgencio Batista.

Ernesto's adventure had turned out to be a path to knowledge. It had also developed another crucial part of his personality, to do with the rites of friendship. In

Bolivian Indians, or *cholos*, amongst the poorest peasants in Latin America, won new rights as a result of the 1952 agricultural reform. When Ernesto reached Bolivia he found a revolution in progress.

that small, sharing community, Ernesto became a man, without ever losing his boyish qualities. In practice, his personality tended to define itself in relation to his friends, and subsequently to his subordinates, who made up a company of independently-minded men. Gallantry and courage retained a certain exhibitionist quality; part of the friendly rivalry some see as importantl to the male identity. Che's jokes, bets, and communications were colored by the heavy irony that characterizes Argentinian humor. The cult of vigor and courage had reached deep into him, both as an ethic and as an aesthetic – resulting in a collection of images. He would frequently reproduce those images for the camera, comparing them with his other, inner mirrors. Perhaps that is the hidden secret in the *Mambo-Tango* photo? It can also be found in the light of those male codes, which he refined almost to dogma, with no room for ambiguity. This attitude explains why friendship would become so important to his future. At the same time it would also make him vulnerable, since it meant that when he met Fidel, he accepted another person's ambitions as his own.

Ernesto Guevara was now close to undergoing another rebirth. In Guatemala he would be given a new name and a new future. Ironically, he

was only able to make the trip thanks to a free passage on a cargo ship belonging to the United Fruit Company. In his usual half-serious joking vein, he wrote to his Aunt Beatriz: 'I have vowed before a print of Stalin, our old and much lamented comrade, that I will not rest until I have seen these monsters annihilated.' Although he eventually chose rural Cuba as the setting for the revolution, only the cities would bring him the result he wanted. Anachronism still found a place in the character of a man who was to become one of the central figures of the 20th century.

In Guatemala City, the 'aimless drifter' experienced two events that provided a framework for his experience. The first was when he witnessed the enemy – the US – in action, which helped to turn his anti-imperialist feelings into an organic ideology. The second came immediately afterwards, in Mexico, where he met the man who would give political direction to that ideology: his quintessential friend, Fidel Castro.

A photograph of Ernesto taken half-way through the journey, when he needed to renew his passport.

Ernesto was moved by the protest marches organized by the miners' popular militias in July 1953 when he arrived in La Paz.

A protest march in Havana, 1952. The
students were protesting against the coup
carried out by Fulgencio Batista.

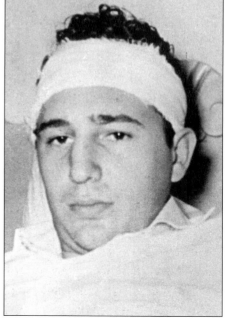

Fidel Castro: the
effects of a day
of violence.

CUBA IS SUFFERING FROM A CRUEL AND IGNOMINIOUS

DESPOTISM, AND YOU WILL NOT BE UNAWARE THAT

RESISTING DESPOTISM IS A LEGITIMATE ACT.

Fidel Castro, 'History Will Absolve Me'.

Guerrilleros in the making.
In the center, Raúl Castro;
Ernesto first on the right,
in dark shorts.

A FEW CUBAN LADS,

REVOLUTIONARIES, ASKED ME IF

I WANTED TO HELP THEIR

MOVEMENT BY USING MY

MEDICAL 'SKILLS', AND I

AGREED, BECAUSE THAT'S THE

SORT OF JOB I'D LIKE TO DO.

Letter to Tita Infante, October 1956

Che the opportunity on 18th June to witness the clandestine US invasion of Guatemala from across the Honduran border. He even signed up as a volunteer with a people's defense brigade and took a training course in shooting. But these were gestures that only led to disappointment, since the Arbenz government reversed its earlier decision to arm the people. It soon became clear that the government would not take matters to their final conclusion. In the end a negligible number of mercenaries were able to lead an invasion and oust a President who had lost the support of his army.

The effect of these events was to convert Che from being a semi-detached fellow traveler into a convinced Soviet supporter. As he wrote to his Aunt Beatriz: 'I have taken a firm stand alongside the Guatemalan government and within the government with the Guatemalan Labor Party, which is communist.' It was also the only party prepared to support Arbenz.

According to Rojo, during the week of the coup the Argentine ambassador, Nicasio Sánchez Toranzo – a genuinely friendly fellow who provided them with *maté* – ran to Che's boarding house early one morning, saying: 'You have to come with me at once. I've been told that there's an Argentinian on the list of agitators to be executed – and it's you.' This diplomatic rescue was in fact unique, since Che was free to come and go from the Embassy as he pleased. Perón's nationalist government was one of the few that firmly supported Arbenz, so the Argentine mission became a refuge for many activists, including several veterans of the assault on the Moncada Barracks

Although the experience of the coup was at the heart of his political development, Che retained a certain youthful immaturity, a sense of pure delight in revolt that colored his ideology. Shortly after the invasion, he told his relatives that in those days he'd had 'more fun than a monkey,' and that he had felt steeped in a 'magical sensation of invulnerability'. 'Everything was great fun here,' he said 'With shooting, bombing, speeches and surprises that cut right through the monotony we'd been experiencing before.' That expression of rebellious joy is a reflection not just of Che's age, but also of the ferment of the times.

The end of 1954

Che Guevara was walking across the Plaza de las Tres Culturas in Mexico City. Around his neck was the camera he used to photograph children and tourists in order to make a living. In March he got a job as a photographer with the *Agencia Latina* agency to cover the Pan-American Games. By this time he had finally got back together with Hilda, which made his lack of money and prospects all the more worrying. He won a scholarship to study under Dr Mario Salazar Mallén at the General Hospital, but still held on to his dreams of more traveling and adventure. He was living in the eye of an approaching tornado – at the heart of a 'big bang' that could shoot him off in any direction.

When the storybook hero finally came to the crossroads, he hoped he would know which path to take.

November 1955.
Che and Hilda Gadea,
a honeymoon couple.

The attack on the Moncada Barracks in Cuba's second city, Santiago, on July 26th 1953 had overturned the political chessboard in Central America. Ever since his 1933 coup, Fulgencio Batista had governed Cuba from the sidelines through a series of appointees. In 1952 he had 'come forward' to govern the country in person. As such, he provided an absolute guarantee of the security of North American interests on the island. Having been one of the first territories to be conquered by Spain, Cuba was also the last nation to

Che, dressed in white, with the Cubans detained in the Miguel Schultz prison.

Che's report card from the 'revolutionaries' academy' could not have been better. Bayo referred to Che as his most disciplined and combative student. Fidel's deep affection for him was beyond any doubt and in April, he appointed Che to be the head of personnel in the house where the recruits were staying.

Although Che's inability to submit himself to institutional life did not reveal itself in the training camp, it soon became apparent in the subtler and more intricate institution of his marriage. The dissolving of a bond which he had only managed to sustain by reading Karl Marx dated back to those months. In a letter to his friend Tita in March, Che broke the news that although Hildita's birth had taken some of the pressure off an 'almost disastrous matrimonial situation', his own 'incapacity to live with her mother' was stronger than the tenderness he felt for his daughter. However, even though the marriage had clearly become an obstacle to him, he was still not quite ready to decide on his future.

In the same letter he confessed that his dearest

Ernesto proudly presents his 'little indian' in the prison yard, June 1956.

53

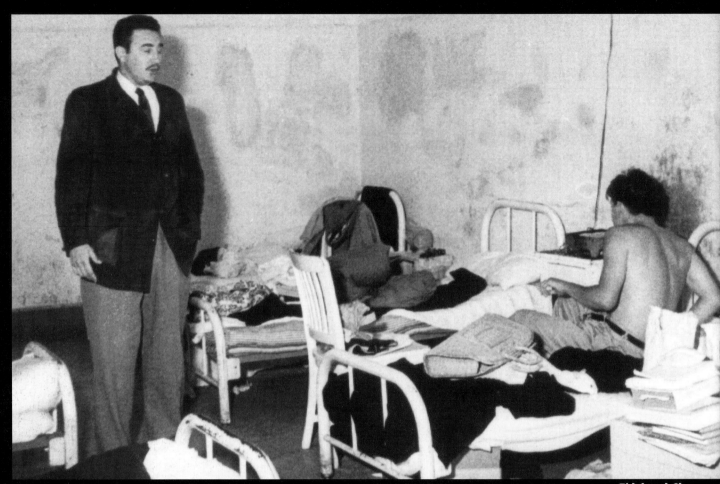

project was to continue living a bohemian life until further notice and 'to land with my sinful bones in Argentina, where I must do my duty by abandoning my wandering knight's cape and taking up some weapon of combat'. It was still not clear whether he would continue in this mood of rootlessness or settle down in the homeland of the *moncadistas*.

In June, as a neighborly favor to the Cuban dictator, the Mexican police detained the members of the July 26th Movement and held them in the Miguel Schultz prison. Che managed to get a letter to Celia de la Serna confirming his political determination: 'I'm no Christ and no philanthropist... I'd fight with every weapon within my reach before I let them nail me to a cross.' A number of pictures from those days in jail survived the saga of the Cuban Revolution. One of them shows Castro and Che in a large communal cell. Standing, wearing a jacket and tie, *El Jefe* – The Chief, Fidel – watches Che put on a shirt: he has the air of a prison guard, an older brother, or a defense lawyer, or perhaps just the quickest at getting dressed. The hierarchy is clear and embodied in Che's unfinished body, the hairless chest and thin arms that would enable his friends to identify him among the dead in Vallegrande.

In spite of the help it received from the Mexican government, the Batista regime was running out of people to talk to. Some sectors of the US government were watching with curiosity the growth of the July 26th Movement – which for the time was keeping to its liberal roots. Fidel had solid support in Havana and once again managed to win his release from prison. He

AT THAT TIME ERNESTO LOOKED RATHER BOHEMIAN, AND HAD A GOOD SENSE OF HUMOR, IN THAT PROVOCATIVE, ARGENTINE STYLE. HE DIDN'T WEAR A SHIRT, WAS RATHER NARCISSISTIC, QUITE DARK-SKINNED, MEDIUM HEIGHT AND STRONGLY BUILT, SMOKED A PIPE AND DRANK *MATÉ*; HE WAS HALF ATHLETIC AND HALF ASTHMATIC, AND USED TO SWITCH BETWEEN STALIN AND BAUDELAIRE, AND FROM POETRY TO MARXISM.

Carlos Franqui. Cuba, el Libro de los 12 ['Cuba, the Book of the 12'].

Castro acted as lawyer for all the detainees.

"A young Cuban leader invited me to join his movement, which wants to bring about the armed liberation of his country. I accepted, of course." Letter to his father.

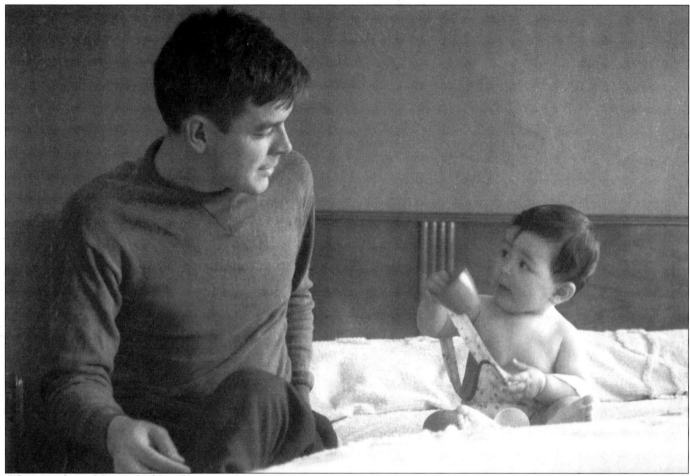

"The most heartfelt petal of love".
Hildita with her father.

"To Hilda, so that on the day of our parting you may inherit the essence of my ambition for new horizons, and my combative fatalism."

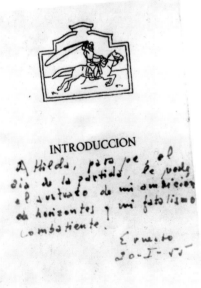

then offered a proof of his loyalty that inspired Che with total confidence in his leader. Moments before he was released from jail, *El Jefe* spoke with Che, who recommended that he should forget about everyone still under arrest rather than delay his plans any further. Che wrote at the time: 'I remember Fidel's response: it was "I will not abandon you." It's the personal attention Fidel gives to the people he cares for that explains why he attracts such fanatical support.' Che was freed on July 31st and resumed his training. In a final undated, letter, written in October or November, he told Tita of his last waverings. The question on his mind at the time was how much uncertainty he could cope with and how viable he thought Fidel's dream might be.

1956

In the early hours of November, 82 men dressed in working clothes boarded a small yacht in the port of Tuxpan, south of Tampico. Che was traveling as the medical officer. The *Granma*, (short for Grandmother) which Fidel had bought from US entrepreneur Robert Erickson, barely had room for 25 passengers and seemed better suited for American pensioners on a slow cruise around Florida than for mounting a rebel invasion. The yawning gap between the rebels' objectives and their limited resources gave the endeavor its epic character.

Seven days of heavy seas in the Gulf of Mexico caused considerable damage to the boat. Many of those on board were ill as a result of the overcrowding, diarrhea and sea-sickness and there was barely enough food and fuel. Years later, on the national holiday that recalls those times, when an attempt was made to squeeze 82 students into the *Granma* there was not enough room for them all to sit down at the same time.

The rebel force finally reached the coast in the early morning of December 2nd, at a point that had not been in their original plans and where there were no signs of the logistical support they were counting on for their landing. A storm pushed the little boat towards the Belic mangrove swamp, on the south of the island, where the rebels found themselves in a marshy labyrinth.

'That was no landing', said Che. 'That was a shipwreck.'

With hindsight, for the invasion force to have reached Cuba at all seems like a triumph of good luck. Fidel suggested that it proved how one person's willpower can attract good luck to his side. Che's response took the form of a maxim: 'Be realistic. Pursue the impossible.'

(left) Fidel, Camilo Cienfuegos, Raúl Castro and Che, setting off for Cuba in the *Granma* (below). "From now onwards, I'd hardly even consider my death to be a set-back. Instead, all I'll take to the tomb will be the regret of an unfinished song."

THE SIERRA IN ARMS

Although the landing of the rebel force did not conjure the symbolism of the Sierra Maestra from thin air – the region had already won its place in Cuban history – there is no question that Fidel Castro reinvented it and in time let its name stand for the beginning of a national triumph.

While the *guerrilleros* were struggling across the swamp, the army concentrated on closing off their route to the hills. Fidel's volunteers had landed in the least populated area of the island. Most of the Oriente (eastern) region – and the Sierra Maestra in particular – was very rural. This meant at first the rebels could not count on the support of the peasants – though their assistance at a later stage provided the key to victory. For the time being they had to stay clear of any local settlements, and were reduced to hunting and fishing for their food.

The rebels came under fire at the first of their staging points, Alegría del Pío, after a peasant tipped off the authorities. The attack sent them dashing to escape through the sugarcane. Twenty-one of Fidel's men were killed in the battle. Che, who was wounded twice, ended up with a group of eight fighters led by Captain Juan Almeida Bosque, the only black man in the rebel command. In the middle of the jungle, uncertain of their next move and harassed by the army, they tried to regroup. The general confusion forced Che to make a choice that reflected changes in outlook which had taken place over a period of time and which he would later see as decisive: 'It may have been the first time I was clearly faced with choosing between my duty to medicine and my duty as a revolutionary soldier.' Since he could only carry one backpack at a time, he was forced to choose between the one crammed with medical supplies and the one which held the ammunition.

'Little beaches and the "Granma"', by Alejandro Aguilera, 1988.

Crescencio Pérez – a *Guajero* (peasant) strongman, with Fidel – brings the *Granma's* survivors news of the solidarity offered by the peasants in the Sierra.

HERE, FROM THE MANIAGUA DISTRICT OF CUBA, LIKE A REAL SOLDIER (AT LEAST I'M DIRTY AND SCRUFFY), I'M WRITING THIS LETTER WITH THE HELP OF AN ARMY PLATE FOR A DESK, A RIFLE AT MY SIDE, AND A NEW ADDICTION BETWEEN MY LIPS: A CIGAR.

Letter to Hilda Gadea, the first since he left.
28 January 1957.

Batista's troops were warned that the rebels had landed.

The Cuban dictator, Fulgencio Batista.

THREE TIMES HE WAS GIVEN UP FOR DEAD, THREE TIMES WE RECEIVED NEWS THAT HE WAS STILL ALIVE, WITH A FEW LINES JUST TO REASSURE US. WE AGED QUICKLY DURING THOSE TWO YEARS. EVERY TIME, I WAS RELIEVED TO KNOW THAT HE WAS STILL ALIVE, THEN I BEGAN TO GIVE UP HOPE AGAIN, KNOWING HOW LONG IT ALWAYS TOOK FOR NEWS TO REACH ME.

Celia de la Serna, 1961.

Ernesto as a character in a cartoon strip. Breccia and Oesterheld illustrate the moment when Che was wounded in the neck. December 5th 1956.

He decided to take the second pack. With that single action, the group's medical officer knew that his future had switched onto a different track. The Argentine novelist, Julio Cortázar, subsequently recreated that period of waiting for the rendezvous with Fidel in his short story *Reunión*. When the survivors were finally able to regroup, there were only 20 of them left.

Other members of the group confirmed that they had lost their only medical supplies with the backpack. One of the group joked that he was relieved at the news since 'Che is a marvelous revolutionary, but a murderous medic', recalling how the doctor had poured iodine directly over the mud-caked foot wounds of one of the injured men.

Che somehow managed to send a letter to his mother, which she received on the last day of 1956. In an allusion to the seven lives that speakers of Spanish attribute to cats, he wrote 'I've used up two and have five left.' The first months of the guerrilla struggle had been spent in attempting to survive, but 'the medic' had found time to become the first chronicler of the Sierra. His diaries were subsequently revised in light of the victory and published years later as *Episodes of the Revolutionary War*.

The first major attack by the *barbudos* (men with beards), as they came to be known, took place on January 17th 1957. It was made against the La Plata Barracks, situated at the foot of Mount Turquino. This was the setting for Che's first act of heroism, as he ran through the bullets without any cover and managed to set fire to a hangar. The 2,000 meter climb up the mountain – the highest on the island – must have been an excruciating effort for the asthmatic, who had run out of inhaler refills.

In the late 1950s, politics came to depend more and more upon ability to communicate with the people as a form of power. In this sense the rebels began with what today might be called 'a serious press problem'. The official news services had already given up Fidel for dead, thereby robbing the guerrilla group of their credibility in Cuba and abroad. To counter these rumors, on February 17th, Castro invited Herbert Matthews of the *New York Times* to meet him in the Sierra. During the Spanish Civil War, Matthews had drawn the criticism of US conservatives for his unconcealed Republican sympathies. Now, since he happened to be in Havana, Fidel was finally able to make a public announcement of the insurgency. His euphoria led him to considerably overstate the human resources behind the Revolution and to launch his first challenge to the White House, asking the journalist to report that 'the weapons your government gives to Batista are not used to defend the hemisphere, as they claim, but against the people'.

Dear oldies: I'm fine, I've used up two and I've got five left... Teté. [Che]"
December 31st 1956.

Che, wearing a helmet belonging to Batista's army.

The Rebel Army and the *campesinos*. A coming-together of forces that would prove decisive to the victory.

Fidel, strong and heavily built. His men called him 'The Horse'.

MY FIRST VICTIM WAS PARDO, WHO CAME OUT IN PRETTY GOOD SHAPE. ALL I NEEDED FOR THE SECOND PATIENT, JOEL IGLESIAS, WAS A STICK OF DYNAMITE TO HELP ME REMOVE HIS EYE-TOOTH. IN THE EVENT, HE GOT THROUGH TO THE END OF THE WAR WITHOUT LOSING IT. MY EFFORTS HAD NOT MET WITH SUCCESS.

Ernesto "Che" Guevara, *Pasajes de la guerra revolucionaria.* ("Episodes from the Revolutionary War")

The success of the group's military action at Turquino allowed them to launch a second attack, at Arroyo del Infierno. It was here that Che killed his first enemy. Fidel rewarded him for his behavior under fire with the privilege of participating with Raúl Castro and Juan Almeida Bosque in the decisions taken by the tactical command. He was no longer 'just another lieutenant'.

During the course of 1957 the rebels won the confidence of the peasants living in the Oriente region. So many of them joined as volunteers that at first there weren't enough weapons to go round. This show of support gave the insurgents a new public platform and a guarantee that they would have all the supplies they needed to survive. Also crucial was the renowned *Radio Bemba* – the informal information circuit – which helped to give the guerrillas credibility and a social base to support their project for seizing power.

Contact with the rural population of the Sierra gave rise to the first legend associated with Che. At the time he was building up a network of peasant supporters and sympathizers, who were becoming progressively more committed to the Revolution. The young lieutenant, who was also a physician and had a foreign accent, found time in the middle of a war to heal the peasants and preach the alphabet. Nor did he miss the chance to try his hand as a dentist – or tooth-puller. For the peasants, he took on the aura of a humane guerrilla, who combined physical endurance with a level of education unknown in the region. A possible hypothesis to explain this response is that in Cuba, a country of very tactile people who like to touch everything they see, Che stood out because of the way he switched back and forth between closeness and distance, between being quietly reserved one moment and eloquent the next. His white skin and unhurried speech also made him a guerrilla with style and – in a land with a mixed-race population – the rarity value of being a citizen of the River Plate. In Havana, following the victory, his good luck and charm also prompted local people to make the cultural link between Che and the leading actors they knew from the Argentine films that had been showing in Cuba for decades.

In March, Fidel faced the necessity of setting up a training school for *guerrilleros*. The intention was to ensure that every volunteer would be trained in the same combat techniques and above all to bring

The dentist, in profile, with one of his "patients".

together groups that came from different backgrounds and had so far been working on their own. The strength of Fidel's guerrillas in the Oriente had already begun to increase now other groups were beginning to ready themselves. The Revolutionary Directorate of Fauré Chomón, for example, had carried out attacks in 'the Plains', as the cities were often called. The Popular Socialist Party (PSP) led by Félix Torres, one of the few Communist parties in Latin America to achieve mass support, also took part in the urban insurgency, though since it still viewed Fidel with some mistrust, it preferred to do so on its own. Meanwhile, Frank País, who had supported the *Granma* effort from the outset, was successfully recruiting volunteers in Santiago.

In the middle of July 1957, Fidel promoted Che to Captain and entrusted him with forming a new (Fourth) column. Shortly afterwards, he decided to reward him again by confirming that he was one of his most trusted followers. He was dictating the signatures to go at the end of a collective letter to Frank País and when he came to the name Guevara, he casually said, 'Put him down as *Comandante*.' And so Che had won his golden star – ahead of Raúl Castro and Juan Almeida. It fell to Celia Sánchez, Fidel's secretary and personal assistant, to pin the star to his black beret.

According to the French biographer, Jean Cormier, Che's gunmaker had been asked to make the star, but had not been told who it was for. This badge of command, the size of small coin, gave Che a form of iconic immortality. It would also become the conceptual center of many of the pictures that were taken of him and of later artistic manipulations of those images. After his death, the famous photo by Alberto Korda would elevate Che's military rank to a mythological status, as if it were the outer token of the *guerrillero*'s ardent heroism. The star, like a third eye, acted as a counterpoint to the true center of the portrait, which was Che's absorbed gaze. The five-point star was also beamed out from Havana as the symbol of an ideology and a political project. Throughout the 1960s and 1970s, it recalled Che's absence and symbolized the Guevarist inspiration behind a wide range of Latin American guerrilla groups – a symbol to compare with the red flag of Communism, or the red carnation of European Socialism.

The golden star of José Martí now began to play its

The cigar as an antidote to asthma and mosquitoes.

Fire in the Sierra.
The star indicates Che's military rank.
On July 21st 1957 he was promoted to
the rank of *comandante* (major).

own part in Che's story. Sparkling in a camera flash or a ray of sunlight, the metal created effects of diffused light that reflected Che's uniqueness. One of the classic images of Fidel and his comrade finds them both sitting at a folding table, engaged in a dialogue about strategies. Che is waiting expectantly while Fidel lights another *habano* (Cuban cigar). Everything in that photograph sparkles: the match flame lighting the cigar is echoed in the star, which is also aflame and sparkles against the beret like a jewel on velvet. Che and Fidel: the ideas and their organization; the fount of the ideology and the master of the political moment. And, passing between them, the ebb and flow of history – as if between the two sides of a single mind.

On May 28th 1957, the rebels launched an attack on the coastal base at Uvero. According to Che, this was the toughest battle of the entire Sierra Maestra campaign. Of 140 combatants, 100 came through unscathed, leaving 40 either dead or wounded. In Uvero, thanks to his even-handed treatment of the injured on both sides, the legend of Che continued to grow. He was known for never killing if it could be avoided. He took no pleasure in physical cruelty and exercised strong moral pressure over his troops to follow his example.

The battle of Uvero, which was widely reported in the press, had a

Women guerrilla fighters. Haydée Santamaría is followed by Celia Sanchez, Fidel's closest friend, and partner.

FIDEL AND ERNESTO STARTED TO WORK OUT THEIR PLANS BY SCRATCHING ON THE GROUND WITH A STICK. IT SEEMS AS IF THEY WERE PLANNING TO BUILD HOSPITALS, SCHOOLS, AND ROADS, BECAUSE THEY LEFT ANY AMOUNT OF SCRATCHES IN THE MUD.

'Old Chana', a countrywoman from the Sierra.

The military strategists' sand table.

AS THE MULE CAME NEARER I COULD SEE THERE WAS A PISTOL HANGING FROM CHE'S WAIST, WITH A LEATHER CARTRIDGE BELT CRAMMED FULL OF BULLETS. TWO MAGAZINES FULL OF CARTRIDGES PROTRUDING FROM THE TWO POCKETS IN HIS SHIRT, AND A CAMERA HANGING AROUND HIS NECK; ON HIS ANGULAR CHIN I COULD MAKE OUT A FEW STRANDS OF HAIR THAT WERE STRUGGLING TO BECOME A BEARD.

Jorge Masetti,
Los que luchan y los que lloran ('Those who fight, and those who cry.')

With his mule, Balansa, in the El Hombrito.

The other battle.
Che recovering from
an asthma attack,
dog in arms.

drink *maté*. His relatives in Havana deny that it was sent to him by his Aunt Beatriz, the beloved relative back in Buenos Aires who devoted her life to compiling newspaper clippings about her nephew. Ana María Erra, Guevara Lynch's second wife, recalls that Che had the gall to ask for *maté* from a certain uncle on the Lynch side of the family who worked as the naval attaché in the Argentinian Embassy in Havana and was a personal friend of Batista. Whatever the case, *maté* was the *Comandante*'s only whim and it arrived at the camp with the same regularity as the dispatches he received from Fidel.

Che's more private moments, given over to what might be termed his 'inner monologue', were chiefly spent with the books he read through methodically, in an attempt to counterbalance action with intellectual effort. According to Vicente de la O, a doctor and an officer in the column, 'He was a tireless reader. He used to open a book when we stopped, while the rest of us, dead tired, closed our eyes and tried to sleep.' Others recall that in the middle of a battle, if he wanted to quickly regain his strength, he would fall fast asleep for half an hour in the shade of a tree.

We return now to the war, this time in the cities. A general strike planned for April 9th failed to take place. Although Fidel had ordered the strike, it was supposed to be carried out by the National Command of the M-26. The defeat cost the lives of many urban comrades. Analyzing this

In May 1958 the Rebel Army's General
Command established its base in La Plata.

Che. A rest break on the trail,
without losing his sense of style.

outcome in the light of his now firmly established opinion of the peasants, Che described it as due to the 'high-risk politics' played by the labor leaders. Following this failure, in *Episodes of the Revolutionary War* he underlined the fact that 'only one person with leadership ability emerged, the leader who was leader in the Sierra, and more specifically, an extraordinary leader – Commander-in-Chief. Fidel Castro.' The military struggle became hegemonic in its efforts to overthrow the dictatorship. The great deeds of the moment were not those of the students or the workers, who for the time being limited themselves to providing political support: they were carried out by Fidel's men. It was June 1958.

Having won a political victory against the strike, the Batista dictatorship launched a massive offensive in the mountains. Ten thousand regular soldiers arrived by land and by sea from every corner of the island. The rebels – who numbered no more than 320 – were forced to confront a tactical problem at the heart of guerrilla warfare: how to turn an eminently defensive situation into a war of attrition. Fidel took personal command of the resistance. Che would have given anything to be on the front line, but Fidel kept him back, reserving him for a prominent role that he planned – or imagined – he might need him to fill at any moment. Although the Army took up a position just seven kilometers from the command post in La Plata, Batista's soldiers seemed to be irreversibly demoralized. The struggle dragged on for two and a half months. During this time the back-and-forth fighting rewarded the rebels with small and gradual gains, but a decisive stash of arms. Fidel and his rebels ended up capturing 400 of the enemy and leaving a further 1,000 dead on the battlefield.

In late August 1958, when Che had just turned 30, Fidel entrusted him with a risky mission. Two of the *Comandante*'s talents weighed heavily in Fidel's decision: Che's daring and his intellectual authority. Both would be crucial if he was to quickly train all the new recruits needed to swell the rebel ranks. With just 140 men under his command, Che set out to conquer half a country.

Che, for once, dressed like a soldier.

21 AUGUST: MILITARY ORDER: *COMANDANTE* ERNESTO GUEVARA IS INSTRUCTED TO LEAD A REBEL COLUMN FROM THE SIERRA MAESTRA TO THE PROVINCE OF LAS VILLAS AND OPERATE WITHIN THAT TERRITORY IN ACCORDANCE WITH THE STRATEGIC PLAN...

Fidel Castro Ruz.

"Get off the sidewalk/ look out or I'll flatten you / here comes Che Guevara / taking on the world." A Cuban song for a Major who speaks with an Argentine accent.

NEXT STOP SANTA CLARA

Batista's offensive had failed. His soldiers had been demoralized by the guerrillas' tactics of continually harrying them and wearing them down while avoiding head-on confrontations. Now the rebel command needed to capitalize militarily on the Army's retreat from the Sierra Maestra. With the rebels in control of the 'liberated territory' of the south, the country was practically divided between two rival régimes. Castro knew that he had to gain control of the cities. It was thought very likely that the dictatorship would draft some formal change in the distribution of power, to try and restore the Army's lost lustre. Even if that failed to win them over, it might

'Rebel Radio'. Che, haranguing and explaining

at least deter them from siding with the rebels. Fidel's plan, referred to as 'the invasion', called for a guerrilla advance to the north-west, drawing two lines across the center of the country in a pincer movement. Those two columns would eventually meet up to attack the army bases closest to Havana.

The advance began on August 31st. At the head of the Eighth Column, renamed *Ciro Redondo* in honor of a fallen fighter, Che set out with his 140 rebels – mostly raw recruits – to conquer what was referred to as the Western Operational Area. His objective was to gain control of the heart of the territory and take over the country's communications. The city of Santa Clara, with a population of 150,000, was the center of the country's rail system.

The Eighth Column got off to an inauspicious start. The Army had cut off its fuel supply, so the Column set out on foot, with only four horses. The rebels only had half a dozen machine guns and some 50 rifles, so – as at the beginning of the Revolution – the challenge given to each of them was to seize an enemy gun.

★

What Castro had in mind was for Che's column to seize and control Santa Clara, then march on to the capital, meeting up with the forces led by Camilo Cienfuegos, who would set off on a parallel path to the east. Camilo, one of Che's great friends, his alter ego and military peer, had no previous experience of commanding troops on his own. He had set off from Salta de la Providencia at the head of the Second Column. His forces, comprising only 71 guerrillas, were the vanguard of the invasion.

Meanwhile, Batista had gathered a force of 10,000 regular soldiers to hold back the invasion, thus effectively abandoning the entire eastern province to its fate. When he took this decision it was not immediately clear whether he was making a mistake, or being realistic in doubting that his demoralized forces could secure a victory.

A historical revision of this triumph indicates that the glorious success of El Escambray had less to do with the ferocity of the actual engagements than with the extremely challenging circumstances of the march, and the guerrillas' ability to evade and mock the Army's attempts to fence them in. In the most spectacular success of his military career – the feat that gave rise to the myth of his invincibility – Che led his raw recruits across the Sierra on foot. According to his own account, 'the only way to make those exhausted men walk was to keep up a barrage of insults, pleadings and every threat you could think of'.

Poachers

The El Escambray campaign represents the other side of Che Guevara's daring. Here his genius consisted not in facing danger but in avoiding it: in refusing to enter into combat with the soldiers strung out along the route. According to Oscar Fernández Mell, a physician and a rebel officer, Che said

A liberator on horseback reaches the Escambray mountains. October 1958.

Che with fighters on Escambray's Second Front, who were most reluctant to accept his leadership.

Following the 'El Pedrero' Pact, Che took over command of all the rebel groups in the Occidente region.

this was not the time for combat but rather for 'fighting nature in order to reach El Escambray'. The key to success in those months consisted in finding a way to keep his impulses in check. The very act of reaching those hills represented a victory, because they had been climbing under fire – although according to Che's own ironic account, 'the Air Force followed our steps mathematically, bombing the scrub land we'd left the day before'.

The famous 'Suicide Squad' dated from those days. It was led by Captain Roberto Rodríguez, nicknamed *El Vaquerito* ('the Little Cowboy') because of his height. Che himself wrote that 'the Suicide Squad was an example of revolutionary morality and only selected volunteers were invited to join it. Nevertheless, every time a man died – which happened in every battle – when a replacement was named, it was distressing to see those who weren't chosen; some of them even cried. It was strange to see these hardened and noble *guerrilleros* showing their youth by spilling tears because they wouldn't have the honor of being first in line to fight and die.' When the Little Cowboy was eventually killed, Che said it was if he had lost 100 men.

In contrast to these heroes was another squad which he referred to as 'the shirtless ones' in a sarcastic reference to the Peronist workers who had fallen into disgrace after the overthrow of General Perón. The group was made up of drunks and rebels suspected of being trouble-makers and

Both photos are taken from the same film. Ernesto, seen through the doorway of the *bohío*, or hut, as he watched the departing *mambí* (rebel) for a long time.

A VETERAN OF THE WAR OF INDEPENDENCE CAME TO BRING US VALUABLE DOCUMENTS. THIS *MAMBÍ* PRESENTED HIMSELF TO THE MAJOR WEARING HIS MEDALS. HE REPRESENTED THE CONNECTION BETWEEN TWO WARS OF LIBERATION, AND WE WERE ALL DEEPLY MOVED. WITH THE CAMERA CHE HAD GIVEN ME, I TOOK THE SHOT OF THE VETERAN FROM INSIDE THE HUT, SO THAT CHE'S HAND IS SHOWING. THEN I WENT OUTSIDE TO TAKE HIS PICTURE WHILE HE WAS DRINKING HIS *MATÉ*.

Antonio Nuñez Jiménez provided the story behind these pictures.

With Victor
Bordón, of the
M-26 guerrilla
movement. Che
cheered up the
troops: "In Havana
they're going to
lay out a red
carpet for us."

The *guajeros* (peasants) join up with an army that also finds time to make a start on its agrarian reform program.

Che giving orders to disarm the enemy soldiers. Fomento, December 18th 1958.

"A pernicious foreigner and a communist leader." The propaganda comes too late: Che is already a mythical figure in Las Villas.

[Poster]
"These are two men who want to lead our young men to their death and destroy our wealth. We are Cubans, not Russians.

We must fight them!

Cuban Civic Youth

CHE GUEVARA
Extranjero pernicioso y Líder Comunista expulsado de la Argentina

CAMILO CIENFUEGOS
Líder Comunista

"Villaclareños"

Estos son los dos hombres que quieren llevar a nuestros jóvenes a la muerte y destruir nuestras riquezas.

Nosotros somos Cubanos y no Rusos.

¡LUCHEMOS CONTRA ELLOS!

JUVENTUD CIVICA CUBANA

cowards. This group, the 'freak show' – considered dispensable – traveled at the rear.

As the troops advanced, Che – like Camilo and the Castro brothers – was also developing ideas for a new de facto economic order with his first attempt at a land reform published on November 8th in the First Decree of the Revolutionary Army. Agrarian reform – 'magic words that mobilized the oppressed masses of Cuba in the struggle for ownership of the land' – called for the nationalization of large land holdings, exemption from taxes for small agricultural producers and the suspension of rent payments. This was an experience that proved to be as crucial for ideologues of the Latin American revolution as it became for officials working in the Cuban government.

At this time, Che had another equally important task to carry out, whose results would help to shape the future of Latin America's first and only Communist nation. In his military orders, Castro had commanded Che to 'co-ordinate operations, plans, administrative and military rulings with other revolutionary forces operating in those provinces... all of which should be brought together to form a single Army Corps.' In other words, he needed to regulate the ideological diversity within the anti-Batista uprising. This would mean narrowing the differences between the original liberal forces of the July 26th Movement, the Revolutionary Command, the fighters on the Second El Escambray Front (who in attempting to claim the territory for

Cabaiguán, a liberated town. Che addresses a large crowd for the first time.

"The Little Cowboy." Che valued "his extraordinary and imaginative way of coping with danger".

themselves had almost come to blows with Fidel's men) and, finally, the pro-Soviet communists of the Popular Socialist Party (PSP), who were somewhat reticent about the ideological independence of Che, 'the foreign officer'. The suspicions were mutual, since Che had his own reservations concerning the Communists: 'In a fraternal discussion I said something to a PSP leader which he then repeated to others as an expression of what at the time he believed to be true: "I can imagine you training cadres who would tear each other apart in the darkness of a prison cell, without saying a word – but you're not capable of training cadres who could storm a machine-gun nest."' The petty resentments and power struggles in El Escambray were finally resolved in the Pact of El Pedrero, which united armed resistance under Che's command. The agreement was signed on December 1st, while they were under air bombardment.

Che recorded the difficulties of continuing with the advance, describing his exhausted troops as 'morally broken, starving... their feet bloodied and so swollen they won't fit into what's left of their boots. They're on the verge of collapse. But in the depths of their eyes you can see a small, faint light, shining in the midst of their desolation.' Famished and tattered, battered by two hurricanes, their feet covered in sores, the troops marched down creeks and across fields of sugarcane like condemned men, crossing rivers, never suspecting that on the other side of the line they would find *el cielo épico* – an 'epic' heaven, and the reward of victory.

They reached the province of Las Villas and on October 16th the Column could finally make out the range of blue hills surrounding Santa Clara. This meant they had at last broken through the circle formed by Batista's forces. They had crossed what on the map looks like a straight line 554 kms long, in a march that lasted 47 days, with just enough food for 20 men. They had marched without knowing how close they were to victory, or that their success would not come as the result of endless bloody battles, but rather through an effort of sheer willpower. It was then that the *Comandante* – in a meeting with the Santa Clara authorities, called to resolve a messy financial situation – met a young underground activist, Aleida March.

Aleida came from Las Villas to Havana in 1957. For years she was an enigmatic figure and her name is not found among the hundreds of chroniclers and witnesses who have written about the Revolution. For a long time she kept the truth of her relationship with Che to herself, enduring his death from a distance, witnessing his enthronement as a founding father and the words of his detractors and his apologists. But in 1996 she broke her silence to tell her story to Jon Lee Anderson, the US biographer.

Aleida had a musical name and wore a skirt that looked black enough and large enough to hide stolen bombs. Born in the province of Las Villas to a family of some education but limited means, Aleida had graduated as a teacher in Santa Clara. The attack on the Moncada Barracks had drawn her into joining the city's underground network and by 1958 she was already one of the M–26's local leaders.

However, Aleida's security cover had been blown in October and the police were searching for her, so the leadership ordered her to hide out in the Eighth Column's camp in El Escambray. Women were not allowed to spend the night in the camp, but the seriousness of

"WHAT ARE YOU DOING HERE?" HE ASKED HER.

"I COULDN'T SLEEP" SHE SAID.

"I'M GOING TO ATTACK CABAIGUÁN", HE SAID.

"DO YOU WANT TO COME?"

"SURE", SHE REPLIED, AND JUMPED INTO THE JEEP.

"AND FROM THAT MOMENT ONWARDS",

SHE RECALLED, WITH A PLAYFUL SMILE,

"I WAS NEVER SEPARATED FROM HIM,

OR LET HIM OUT OF MY SIGHT."

Jon Lee Anderson. Che Guevara: A Revolutionary Life.

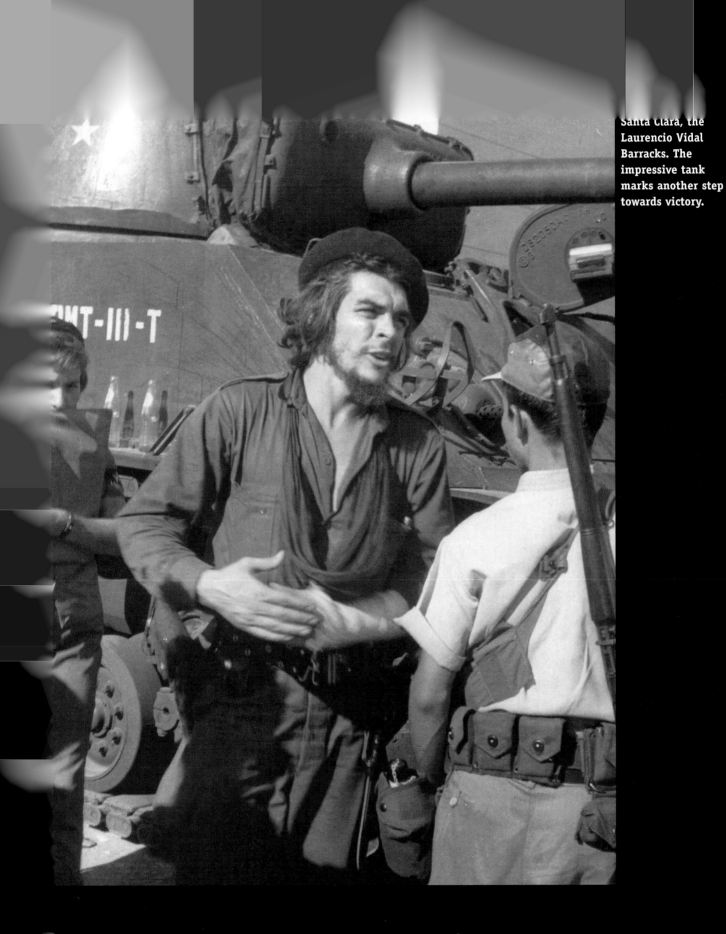

Santa Clara, the Laurencio Vidal Barracks. The impressive tank marks another step towards victory.

The popular forces can win a war against an army, we don't have to wait for the right conditions for a revolution, the insurrection can

Derailment of the armor-plated train and a rebel posing (below), Molotov cocktail at the ready. Aleida March standing by the engine (bottom right). Che might have said to her: "I'm going to take your photograph for history". The rebels had taken Santa Clara.

YOUR STRONG AND GLORIOUS HAND

OPENS FIRE OUT OF HISTORY

WHEN THE WHOLE OF SANTA CLARA

WAKES UP TO SEE YOU.

AND HERE IS THE PROOF,

THE INTIMATE TRANSPARENCY

OF YOUR BELOVED PRESENCE,

COMANDANTE CHE GUEVARA.

Carlos Puebla, "Hasta Siempre".

To the showers! After the fragrancy of combat, Aleida March offers Che a bar of soap.

the situation made the *Comandante* change his mind. Aleida did not have what one might call a docile character and they didn't share the same ideologies, so when Aleida spoke disdainfully of the Communists Che played down the significance of the urban insurgency. According to Aleida's revelations, their's was not a case of love at first sight, but of revolutionary love, sparked off by their proximity in the midst of danger. One night, when she couldn't sleep, she walked out to the road. The major came by with his jeep and offered her a ride, with a typical guerrilla pick-up line: 'I'm on my way to attack Cabaiguán'. Aleida got into the jeep and they carried out the attack. She recalled that 'From that day on I never once left his side.' By early December 1958, at the height of the campaign, they were lovers.

By the end of 1958, military dynamics had changed considerably in both sectors of the island. We now know that the entire revolution was won during those months and that the rebels' final drive coincided with the demoralization of an army that had, in effect, already surrendered. By this stage, even Batista had lost all

88

faith in his armed forces and was chiefly concerned with preparing for his escape. In the morning of December 16th, with only three poorly-armed squads and the rest of his men hidden nearby, Che launched an attack against the Fomento Barracks. He began with one of those gestures so typical of this youthful revolution: telephoning the lieutenant in charge to ask him to surrender. The offer was turned down. The 120 soldiers inside did not know that the enemies surrounding them were even fewer in number. Both sides held out. The Air Force bombed the rebels, who controlled the road between the barracks and the town of Placetas, but they held to their positions and followed Che's bold instructions to keep the barracks under siege. As the hours passed, the regular soldiers lost their enthusiasm for shooting and began to wonder what they were really defending. On December 18th Major Guevara entered the captured barracks. The road was open to Santa Clara.

Following the victory at El Escambray and the attacks carried out under heavy aerial bombardment by Fidel and his brother Raúl in the Oriente region, on December 22nd, Camilo launched an attack on the Yaguajay base in Cruces.

One week later Che launched the siege of Santa Clara by attacking the outlying barracks and seizing the electricity station. By 'liberating' the north-west of the city he was able to take over an important radio station and to announce in person that the city was effectively in the hands of the revolutionaries.

One particularly celebrated episode in the Guevara story was the capture of an armored train carrying weapons and ammunition. According to Che's account, once the rails had been cut, the train was pelted with Molotov cocktails from the nearby Cápiro hills: 'Surrounded by men hurling bottles of burning gasoline from nearby cover and from neighboring wagons, the train – thanks to its armor plating – quickly turned into an oven. In just a few hours every one of the crew surrendered, along with their 22 goods wagons, their anti-aircraft guns and machine guns and their fabulous stocks of ammunition.' Antonio Núñez Jiménez, the rebels' map-maker, who at this time was in Che's column, has denied accounts suggesting that this was less of a heroic attack than a hand-over

> TO REASSURE HIS FAMILY IN LATIN AMERICA AND THE PEOPLE OF CUBA, WE CONFIRM THAT *COMANDANTE* CHE GUEVARA IS ALIVE, AND IN THE FRONT LINE.
>
> *Radio Rebelde refutes Che's death.*

Two fighters keep watch over their major while he sleeps.

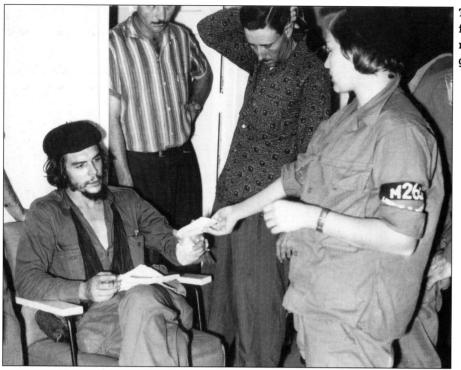

The guerrilla
fighters face a new
responsibility:
governing.

Che was magnanimous with the men
he defeated. Here he offers his hand
to a prisoner.

negotiated between Che and a lieutenant who deserted as soon as he was given some money. However, he confirmed that what happened was not so much a surrender as a derailment that Che's forces were able to turn to their best advantage. The battle of Santa Clara was one of the most decisive victories of the Revolution and heralded the beginning of the end. Although just six guerrillas died there, in the new history of Cuba it has been given as much prominence as the great confrontations of the Wars of Independence. It led to the definitive military and popular coronation of Che, who was hailed by the people as a liberator. He had become the model *guerrillero*.

On the night of January 2nd, the Second Column, proceeding from Yaguajay, reached the newly-liberated city. Major Cienfuegos made his way to the Public Works building, which housed the rebel command in Santa Clara, and gave his friend the orders he had received from Fidel. The meeting between the two front-line columns was celebrated with a dinner in which 600 sandwiches were shared out between all the troops. At dawn the two columns headed out for their final objective: the main barracks outside Havana. Camilo would take the military city of Colombia, while Che would attack the fortress of La Cabaña. Some historians have asked why Fidel would have assigned Colombia – the more difficult military objective – to *Comandante* Cienfuegos, who was third in command – or perhaps fourth, after Raúl Castro – while Che's orders were to take a comparatively uncomplicated objective. While they were saying their farewells, they discussed the latest news which suggested that Batista had fled. Since Fidel, Camilo and 'the well-known Argentinian communist' had themselves been proclaimed dead on so many occasions, they thought they were just hearing another round of propaganda. But this time their own intelligence confirmed that the tyrant had indeed fled the island.

Che had put on some armor plating to protect himself from the Cuban people's tendency to be over-exuberant and light-hearted. not to take life too seriously. When we saw the way he was treated by Camilo we were shocked. I remember one time when Camilo began to pester him. Che looked at him and said "Camilo, don't forget that my men are here as well". Later on, they left together, arm-in-arm.

Luis Báez. Secretos de generales. Testimonio de Enrique Acevedo González.
('Secrets of the Generals: a statement given by Enrique Acevedo')

Castro: 'Now the tanks belong to the people... nobody's going to leave them alone". The women of Havana, dressed patriotically in flags, took him at his word.

DAYS OF GLORY

'The Don Quixote of the Street Lamp', was the title Korda gave to a *guajero* (peasant) enjoying the view.

At dawn on the first day of 1959, Fulgencio Batista climbed aboard the plane taking him into exile. He handed over his command to General Eulogio Cantillo and flew into the arms of the Dominican dictator, Leónidas Trujillo. Until the very last minute Cantillo and the US State Department had been concocting a scheme to prevent the uprising from succeeding. Castro neutralized this threat on Radio Rebelde, with his message to the people: *'Revolución sí, golpe militar no!'* ('Yes' to revolution; 'No' to military coups!')

The English historian, Eric Hobsbawm, puts the victory of the Cuban Revolution in perspective: 'Fidel won because the Batista regime was weak and lacked any real support beyond what was due to convenience and personal interest; also because it was led by a man whose long and corrupt career had made him lazy... Once Fidel had made this clear, it was only logical that his forces would take over the government. A bad government with little support had been overthrown.'

The military objectives given to the leading columns were quite straightforward. Wearing his wide-brimmed hat and his prophet's beard, Camilo made his entry into Havana amid popular jubilation on the morning of January 3rd, 1959. Che arrived early and more discreetly on the following day, wearing his worn-out uniform and a straggly beard. He began to see for himself the capital city of the unknown land he had just liberated.

Fidel's arrival in the capital on January 8th was the culmination of a process of canonization as he made his way from the Oriente region. Havana quickly made a big impression on Che. The first thing he did was to call his father. Che's accent had become more Cuban, to the point that at first Guevara Lynch didn't recognize his voice. 'It's me, old man', he said in a familiar Argentinian greeting. This was enough to bring back their years together. In one unpublished interview, Che said that hearing his father's voice again for the first time in six years had been the most emotional moment he had experienced in those times.

The jeep used by the men with beards: Cienfuegos, Chomon, Fidel, Ramíïro Valdez, Raúl, Ameijeira, and Che, looking as if he's meditating rather than celebrating.

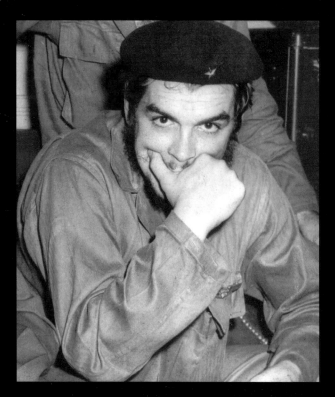

The victory celebration was a drunken affair, in which the Left joined with the traditional parties, the rich with the poor, students with workers – and all to the rhythm of a mambo. These were glory days indeed, with all the effervescence of a carnival. Che crossed Havana on a tank, then on a jeep, with Camilo at his side, sitting next to Fidel, passing before a population celebrating the triumph, drunk with euphoria. And in the streets were the Havana women dressed up like statues of the Motherland, wearing their Phrygian caps[1] and dressed in red and blue, climbing onto the tanks like floats in a carnival parade.

At the heart of this whirlwind came Che's reunion with his family. They arrived on January 9th, on a plane Cienfuegos had sent to Buenos Aires to bring back comrades exiled by Batista. Che's parents had not seen their son since that farewell on the platform of Retiro Station. The pride in Celia's expression reflected a sense

1 A conical hat worn during ancient times that became a symbol of liberty during the French Revolution.

of compensation for her many sleepless nights.

Yet this was not an entirely comfortable victory reunion for Che. Hilda Gadea and his little daughter had also came to visit him and he found himself in the difficult position of having to tell them of his relationship with Aleida March. The photos confirm that Aleida kept as close to him as a bodyguard – but, after all, the Cuban Revolution was hers to celebrate as well. The two of them only slept for one or two hours at night and did not have time to see Havana together. In addition, partly because he was a foreigner, Che could not at first find a place for himself within the revolutionary triumph since the new regime had still not formally taken office.

Fidel's jeep driving through the crowd, in a city paralysed by the general strike.

As the party continued, political developments went on at a dizzying pace and uncertainty ruled. Because Fidel was only 32 years old he was ineligible for the Presidency, and the government had fallen into the hands of President Manuel Urrutia and a reformist cabinet. Since overcoming this impediment meant amending the Constitution, for the time being Fidel could only reconfirm his position as Commander-in-Chief of the rebel forces. With a de facto parallel government, the political situation looked decidedly unstable.

Entering Havana, January 8th 1959. Fidel and Camilo celebrate without letting their guard drop.

Overseas, the same confusion prevailed and the victory was praised from the strangest political positions. In Buenos Aires it was celebrated by the military government. The Left looked sympathetically on Fidel's triumph as proof that the days of Latin America's remaining dictators – Stroessner in Paraguay, Somoza in Nicaragua, Trujillo in the Dominican Republic – were numbered.

Fidel had kept his ties to some people in the US government. After the Revolution's victory, the Conference of Communist Parties of Latin America and the Caribbean declared that what had happened in Cuba effectively banished 'the myth of geographic fatalism, utilized by imperialism and oligarchies to strengthen their repressive yoke'. The Cuban Revolution has survived up to the present day to challenge that

For the family album. Everyone wants a photo with the *guajeros* and their rifles.

Fading smiles from the patrician women, who would soon be packing their bags.

fatalism. At the time, the rebels were convinced that they would make history, drawing strength from their position as a geographic Achilles' heel.

Power equals money

US interests controlled 90 per cent of Cuba's nickel deposits and other mineral resources, 80 per cent of its public services and 50 per cent of the railway network. Together with the UK, they ran the petroleum industry and the great agricultural holdings that accounted for half of the usable land. North American business represented 65 per cent of Cuba's total exports; in addition the country was mortgaged to the hilt. US groups, which preferred not to place all their eggs in one basket and had not been sure if Batista, 'Their Man in Havana', would be there much longer, had made contributions to revolutionary funds during the insurgency. However, within a week of the rebels' triumphant entry into Havana, the US Congress sent out its first aggressive signal – what the newspaper *Revolución* called 'the wake-up call' – by insisting that future Cuban economic plans should not be allowed to harm US capital. Castro's immediate and defiant response foreshadowed the changes that would come in February, when he became Prime Minister.

In the meantime, Che had taken command of La Cabaña, the 18th-century fortress near the capital that had been converted into a military base. The summary judgements on hundreds of Batista's torturers and informers – acts that gave fresh ammunition to Cuban exiles or *gusanos* (worms) and politicians in Washington – date from those turbulent days. The Revolution sentenced the most notorious repressors to the firing squad after quite perfunctory trials. According to which sources are used, the number of executions range from 200 to 1,500. Fidel admitted to 550. Che supervised the executions in Havana, which were carried out in an old moat surrounding the army base. There are no reports of him either seeking vengeance, or displaying humanitarian remorse. The summary executions were in accord with the logic of the Revolution; they were intended to signify the restoration of Justice.

Looking back on those days, it is hard to recall the dizzy pace of events shaping Cuba's future. Every part of the power structure was being rebuilt. This was a

The Havana Hilton, renamed the Havana Libre. The Revolution began to take control of the symbolic places.

I ASKED CHE IF HE WOULD LET ME GO TO THE ORIENTE TO SEE MY FAMILY. HE REPLIED QUITE BRISKLY THAT HE WOULDN'T. I SAID TO HIM, "BUT CHE, WE'VE WON THE REVOLUTION". "NO", HE SAID, "WE'VE WON THE WAR. THE REVOLUTION IS JUST BEGINNING", AND THAT WAS THE END OF THE CONVERSATION.

Statement by rebel soldier, Mustelier.

Che talking to RAI [Argentine International Radio Service], sitting next to Alberto Bayo. Behind, the black man is Pombo, and the last on the right is Rogelio Acevedo.

Secret discussions follow on from the summary indictments. "And if we have to stand up against international opinion, we're ready to do so", said Castro, defiantly.

The Planning Office, staffed by Che and Nuñez Jiménez. It was virtually a secret government, running parallel to that of President Urrutia.

country changing to a new standard, but the standard itself was still in the making – and meanwhile, there was the Cold War which left no room for shadows and ambiguities, especially in countries with economies as dependent as Cuba's. But that sense of dizziness can also be understood from the viewpoint of the Revolution's leaders, who had an average age of 30 and no experience in power. Those stark facts, for which there can have been few historical precedents, only served to speed up the process.

In early February, the Cabinet of Ministers issued a decree granting Cuban citizenship to every foreigner who had fought against the dictatorship. That was how Ernesto Guevara de la Serna came to formally renounce his Argentinian citizenship. At about this time he was forced to take to his bed. The recent struggle had left him with anaemia, and emphysema in both lungs. He was advised to take some rest in the beach resort of Tarará, close to the capital.

In Tarará, Che became an ideologue of the new state. This was where Cuba's future was sketched out, from the fine details of an urgent program of land reform to the first plans for taking the Cuban experience to the rest of the continent, and a new approach to economic and foreign affairs. In those weeks of secret high-level meetings, Che dealt with an agenda of key issues, such as the restructuring of the military (the Revolutionary Armed Forces) and the formation of the new security apparatus and police force. The Revolution would have to learn how to protect what it had won, both at home and abroad. The government drew closer to the old Communist party, the PSP, and by May its leftward movement was confirmed. Washington of course was aware that Che Guevara, Castro's *eminence grise*, was the prime mover behind this program of radicalization,

On February 17th, after Fidel's tour through the US and the most prosperous countries of the continent – Argentina, Brazil and Uruguay – the government announced its proposals for a Land Reform Law. These avoided

Fidel returns from his visit to the United States. The leaders crowd the steps to the plane. May 1959.

OUR REVOLUTION HAS DESTROYED THE

THEORIES OF THE ARMCHAIR STRATEGISTS.

WE HAVE TO BRING ABOUT A REVOLUTION

IN FARMING, AND FIGHT FOR CHANGE

IN THE FIELDS AND THE MOUNTAINS,

AND THEN BRING THE

REVOLUTION INTO

THE CITIES.

Che, January 1960

HE WAS AWARE OF HIS

PERSONALITY, AND WAS

DEVELOPING INTO SOMEONE

WHOSE FAITH IN THE EVENTUAL

TRIUMPH OF HIS IDEALS BEGAN

TO APPROACH MYSTICISM.

Ernesto Guevara Lynch

Reunited with his mother, Celia. The family traveled in a plane bringing back Cubans who had been exiled in Argentina. January 9th 1959.

any rhetoric of violent expropriation and provided significant compensation for confiscated lands. However, to the extent that they proposed to do away with large landholdings, they were seen as damaging to US interests. This forced Che to find a compromise which involved making a number of concessions from his original ideas. The measure was completed with the creation of the National Institute of Land Reform (INRA), a super-charged Ministry of Industry that aimed to mobilize the people in order to produce radical social and economic change. The Institute was intended to draw the peasants closer to the center of the political scene and at the same time Che pressed for literacy projects for the rural population.

No one was surprised when President Urrutia resigned in July. He was succeeded by the socialist Osvaldo Dorticós, who remained in power until 1976.

Even though the cities were not among Che's direct concerns, he was very aware that in addition to ensuring improved opportunities for the peasants,

In Havana Hildita rejoined a father who had become a major. Her doll was a present purchased after Che's friends had made a collection.

other communities would also require various forms of assistance.

Havana had a large and lively middle class and an intellectual élite who were nervously following the course of events. The remarkable film by Tomás Gutiérrez Alea, *Memories of Underdevelopment*, made in 1962, tells of the difficult transition of an intellectual forced to confront the fact that the opposition has taken power. Faced, that is, with the dilemma of either becoming a fully-committed intellectual of the Revolution, or emigrating. At the end of the 1950s, that dilemma suddenly had a solution; now the artistic vanguard went hand-in-hand with the political vanguard and – especially in those arts that directly reflected 'reality' – Marxism sealed up the cracks. At this time photography was where one of the most productive and useful interplays between art and politics took place. Alberto Díaz – nicknamed 'Korda', who was to create the emblematic image of Che – remembered that Cuban photographers had been very frustrated when they were unable to photograph the rebels in the Sierra Maestra. Now suddenly they were all in Havana, walking through the crowds, offering a feast of images. The New Cuban Photography was born in the heat of the Revolution and thanks to its profound identification with its leaders began to develop a spontaneous image of power-in-the-making. Korda became Fidel's photographer and – with other artists, such as Osvaldo Salas and Raúl Corrales – one of the architects of the government's public image. Political leaders and photographers together embarked on a remaking of reality.

Meanwhile, the great Cuban capitalists, the fashionable investors and the old gambling and rum barons were emigrating with their gaudy wives in tow. They settled in Miami (where the Hilton Hotel also came to be called the Havana Libre,) and vainly engaged in conspiracies, waiting for Fidel to fall.

Che's marriage to Aleida March took place as soon as he recovered his health. One of the witnesses was Fidel, who scribbled his signature and left before the cake was cut. The other two were the recently-named police chief, Efigenio Ameijeiras and Raúl Castro, who had been close to Che in his Marxist

WITH YOUR LOVE THAT

SWITCHES ON SUDDENLY,

LIKE A LAMP, IN THE MIDDLE

OF THE NIGHT.

Olga Orozco. No hay puertas.
('There are no doors.')

convictions ever since their time together in the Sierra. Aleida was radiant in white, while her husband looked more like an actor who had wandered onto the wrong set (see p. 104).

1959 marked the beginning of Che's period as an architect of Cuban socialism. Although he had remarried, he was not planning to lead a settled life. He always gave the impression of being uncomfortable with his assigned place, whether as a husband or a minister. Of all Che's unquestionable virtues perhaps the best was his determination never to turn into a bureaucrat. He never accepted any form of institutionalization and his dogged self-sufficiency would always keep him from being a conformist. His outsider status also helped make him such a model of modernity.

There is an unanswered question concerning what political motives might have led Fidel to manage without Che in the first crucial months of the new government. On June 12th, a few days after the wedding, Che set off as Cuba's emissary on his first diplomatic journey, which was a tour of the Third World and Japan. More than once he was introduced as Cuba's vice-president. His itinerary was a sign that the new

The wedding party. The women, dressed up. The men, much as usual.

Ernesto Guevara de la Serna and Aleida March become husband and wife. June 2nd 1959.

Cuba was a state that considered itself to be independent of the great powers, and ready to take its place with other non-aligned nations: the Middle East, India, Southeast Asia, and Yugoslavia, the least Soviet of the socialist countries. Che was able to fulfil some of his traveler's dreams, such as visiting the pyramids and shaking hands with heads of state who had preceded him in liberating their countries. After naming Che 'the great ambassador of the oppressed', Egypt's Gamal Nasser put him up in the palace of the former King Farouk I and showed him the MiG planes and submarines he had bought from the Soviets. Throughout the trip, Che was doing more than sightseeing, or making himself known. He was more like a visitor to a World Fair, gathering new ideas to take home. The same happened in India, where he was received by Jawarlahal Nehru. He was interested in the railroads and in importing Indian-made arms, although that particular request was ignored. No one knew whether his informality and directness as a diplomat was a deliberate tactic or mere candor. He learnt about politics by being overly direct, as when he criticized Nasser's land reform, or asked Nehru's opinion about Mao. In a letter sent from India that has recently been made public, Che shared his intimate thoughts with his mother, revealing that as he became more convinced of the historical role he might play, he felt increasingly constricted by the real, everyday world.

More aeroplanes

Che also made a brief visit to Japan as the model of a

Never alone. Pombo and Hernandez López join the married couple as they leave the house of Alberto Castellanos, where the wedding party had been held.

Photograph by Raúl Corrales, 1959.

I MADE A FLATTERING REMARK TO ALEIDA, AND FROM THE WAY CHE LOOKED AT ME I THOUGHT, "BACK OUT, ALBERTO, YOU'VE GOT NO CHANCE THERE".

Alberto Castellanos, who some months later was best man at the wedding.

Cairo, June 1959. Curiosity and need come together. Everything can be put to use in the New Cuba.

A technical fault in the plane leaves Che "stuck in Madrid". He watches the bull fight, but without showing much enthusiasm.

country that became industrialized in record time. He admired the country's heavy industry, which as the future Minister of Industry would become his area of special concern. Indonesia was another country that seized his imagination, not least because it produced the same basic goods as the Caribbean, such as sugar, coffee and tobacco. His tour ended in Tito's Yugoslavia. Marshal Tito, having successfully resisted German occupation, had broken with Stalin 11 years previously and established a government which offered an alternative form of socialism. Che was able to form a very clear sense of the fragile cohesion of the Balkan federation, which was only held together by the charisma of its leader and his efforts to play down ethnic differences.

Towards the end of October 1959, the Cuban Revolution suffered the loss of a key player. The light plane carrying Camilo Cienfuegos from one province to another vanished without trace, the victim of an accident or possibly of undetected sabotage. Fidel himself took part in the search and rescue flights. Camilo had been an extraordinary *compañero* to Guevara in the conquest of the Occidente (west). Simple, living life to the fullest, wanting nothing more than to be at the center of the action, Camilo counterbalanced Che's thoughtful side. He was his equal however in light-hearted, jokey ways – another boy who never quite grew up. After two weeks of intensive searches, the plane was confirmed as having disappeared. A short time afterwards, when Che published one of his most important works, he dedicated it to Cienfuegos. *Guerrilla Warfare* was an instruction manual for insurgents that he had written at the beginning of the year. Camilo would

Photograph by Osvaldo Salas.

THIS REVOLUTION IS THE FIRST

REAL CREATION THAT CAME OUT

OF IMPROVISATION... THE MOST

PERFECT EXAMPLE OF ORGANISED

CHAOS IN THE WORLD.

Che

THE DAILY
REVOLUTION

'**F**idel's crazy. Every time a Guevara starts a business, it goes broke.' This warning came from the father of the brand-new civil servant. Eleven months after the victory, on November 28th 1959 *Comandante* Guevara was named head of the Cuban National Bank. While Che's recollection of how that event came to pass may not have been entirely accurate, the story did him credit. According to his account, at one point in a high-level meeting, Fidel asked if any of those present was an economist. The *Comandante*, his attention elsewhere, and thinking he had heard 'a communist', raised his hand. And so he was given the job. Herbert Matthews, the *New York Times* correspondent, observed that 'there was amazement and a sense of

Time, August 8th 1960. Che between Kruschev and Mao.

ridiculousness about it... Che knew nothing about banks, but Fidel needed a revolutionary... and there *were* no revolutionary bankers.' Che's story reflected his bitingly anti-bourgeois instincts and also revealed a tendency towards creative improvization that became a feature of those early years.

The first difficulty Che faced as a banker was that he had a deep disdain for money, which he saw as a symbol of exploitation. 'The payment of a salary is an ancient evil... that was born with the establishment of capitalism... and will not even die in the socialist stage,' he wrote in 1962. 'It will [only] disappear with the last dregs; it will run out, you might say, when money ceases to circulate, and we reach the ideal stage: communism.' Che's work at the Bank, where he learnt about finance, as he put it 'by osmosis', forced him to delegate his responsibilities at INRA to another official, Orlando Borrego. After joining the *Ciro Redondo* Column in October 1958, Borrego was magnetized by Che, and in

DARLING HILDITA, ... REMEMBER THAT WE'RE STILL
FACING MANY YEARS OF STRUGGLE, AND THAT EVEN WHEN
YOU'RE A WOMAN, YOU'LL HAVE TO PLAY YOUR PART.
IN THE MEANTIME WE HAVE TO PREPARE OURSELVES, TO BE
VERY REVOLUTIONARY, WHICH AT YOUR AGE MEANS
LEARNING A LOT, AS MUCH AS YOU CAN, AND TO BE READY
ALL THE TIME TO GIVE YOUR SUPPORT TO JUST CAUSES.

Papá

With the film-
maker, Tomás
Gutiérrez, during
filming of *Historias
de la Revolución*,
1960.

Hildita watching the
Revolutionary
Display, standing
between her father
and Nuñez Jiménez.

A famous 3 a.m. meeting between Jean-Paul Sartre and Simone de Beauvoir, in Che's office in the Bank, taken by Korda. In 1997 the photographer came across the second photo by chance, amongst his negatives: the young peasant woman guard had fallen asleep.

Burning warehouses after the explosion on the ship *La Coubre*, carrying Belgian arms. Havana port, 4th March 1960.

remove him as a potential threat, it would reduce the pressure of Che's popularity. From Fidel's point of view, Che would be more useful as a distant shadow than close to hand. Fidel would be quite surgical in doing what he felt had to be done, which meant that the more Che traveled, the better.

The objectives of the new diplomatic mission which began on October 21st 1960 were political as well as economic. Che visited China, the Soviet Union, Czechoslovakia, East Germany and North Korea – in effect, a large part of the Communist world. In the GDR he had to contact a German-Argentinian translator, Tamara Bunke, a committed young communist who was fascinated by the Cuban Revolution. Six months later, she went to Havana to help develop Cuba's plans for armed struggle in Latin America. In Prague, Cuba was offered an easy loan. Wherever Che went, he examined machinery as carefully as if he were a quality control inspector. Given the money, he would have taken everything back with him. When he was in Moscow for the October 1917 celebrations, the Soviets invited him onto the podium, and took him to visit the Presidium, a distinction reserved for the highest government officials. The people of Moscow gave him an ovation in Red Square, and to consummate its grand flirtation, the USSR bought three million tons of Cuban sugar.

Outrage at the bomb blast [see p. 118]. On his way to his office in the Bank, Che passed by the site of the bombing, and spontaneously joined those already there in helping to rescue the victims.

Despite of his success in the USSR, the high point of Che's tour was China. By that time the Russian Premier, Nikita Khruschev, had launched the slogan of 'peaceful coexistence', a bland formula intended to paper over the Cold War. The makeshift peace excluded China, where conflict was already brewing. Beijing accused Khruschev's bureaucrats of doctrinal

A young Korean woman puts the Major's dancing skills to test. Pyongyang. December 1960.

Guevara greeting Mao Zedong at his first official dinner with the Chinese government. December 1st 1960.

"Cuba will have everything it needs": Nikita Kruschev.

The first visit to Moscow, November 1960.

WHEN HE SAID IN RUSSIA THAT
CUBA WAS LACKING IN SOME OF
THE RAW MATERIALS NEEDED TO
MAKE DEODORANTS, THE RUSSIANS
SAID, "DEODORANTS? YOU'RE
USED TO HAVING TOO MANY
CONSUMER GOODS."

Ernesto Cardenal

SOME TRUTHS ARE SO OBVIOUS THAT IT'S POINTLESS TO DISCUSS THEM. BEING A MARXIST IS AS NATURAL AS BEING A NEWTONIAN IF YOU'RE A PHYSICIST, OR A PASTEURIAN IF YOU'RE A BIOLOGIST.

Che

'revisionism'. For Che, coming from an island with a fragile economy and firmly believing in the need for the Left to remain united against US imperialism, the dispute between China and the USSR came as a bitter disappointment. When he arrived in Beijing, a car took him to the historic fortress of the emperors, the Forbidden City. But although Mao lived in the vast complex, Che was not able to greet him personally that morning. Instead, he had to content himself with watching the 'Great Helmsman' drinking tea behind a glass screen, in a bizarre Chinese version of a peep show, and waving to him as a gesture of welcome. However Che did have the chance to talk with senior government officials, including the influential Defense Minister, Lin Piao, whose political writings had some affinity with Che's own works. In the end, he also met Mao at two official dinners. He managed to sell another million tons of Cuban sugar. While he was in Beijing, Aleidita (later called Aliucha) – his first daughter with Aleida March – was born.

Towards the end of 1960, Moscow courted its new Caribbean friend with generous promises and special prices; it offered its trust, and gave signs of doing what it could to help. However, the later course of their

An unconditional approach that does not exclude minor changes: Che was always pressing for a more radical course.

Behind Che is Castro, omniscient. He always had the final word.

relations suggests that this was when the USSR began to tighten the screws on the Cuban economy. Khruschev spoke of setting up 100 factories, and promised to increase Cuban steel production from 40,000 to 200,000 tons a year. Since its US oil contracts had been cancelled, the island could become became a refinery for Soviet crude. This was attractive as Che knew that to concentrate more-or-less exclusively on sugar production would weaken the Cuban economy. As a result, there were two projects which kept him up at night: industrialization and agricultural diversification.

Moscow's deference to its visitors, and the international trips made by Che and other high-ranking Cuban officials, were followed with unease in the West. In the US, the press already spoke of Che as 'the czar of the Cuban economy' and 'the brains behind Castro'. However US foreign policy was not supported by the election results and so, before leaving the White House in 1959, Republican President Dwight Eisenhower planned an invasion of the island. The plans were completed on January 3rd, when diplomatic relations with Cuba were severed. Both measures put pressure on Eisenhower's successor, the Democrat John F Kennedy. Sabotage attempts multiplied in Cuba, with fires in the sugar fields and bombs in several factories. It was clear that the State Department supported the anti-Castro émigrés in Miami, and coordinated their sabotage operations with opposition activists in Cuba. The government and the whole country lived in a state of fear, realizing that the Pentagon had drawn up an invasion plan.

The US had intervened in Cuba three times at the beginning of the century. But to Che the invasion at the Bay of Pigs on the central coast

"Militias in the Malecón".
This photo, by Corrales, records the
historic moment when 200,000 Cubans
were mobilised to defend every possible
landing point against an enemy invasion.

(Playa Girón, as it came to be known in Cuban history) must have seemed familiar as it had a lot in common with the attack on Guatemala that he had witnessed in 1954. On April 15th 1961, US B-26 bombers piloted by Cuban exiles bombed the air bases at Santiago, San Antonio de los Baños and Ciudad Libertad. These missions prepared the way for the main operation two days later. Having trained in Guatemala, with the approval of dictator Miguel Ydígoras Fuentes, some 1,500 anti-Castro fighters from Miami, Puerto Rico and Nicaragua landed at Girón to set up a beachhead. Che was stationed in Pinar del Río, protecting Havana and the west of the island, where they were expecting a major attack. Fidel dispatched 3,000 soldiers to the bay where the *gusanos* – 'worms' as the Cuban exiles came to be known – had landed, to prevent them from consolidating their beachhead. Fidel personally supervised the defense, and the whole island drew together to resist the invaders. The Revolution was too fresh in people's minds to have lost its appeal, and thousands of volunteers came forward. From the beach at Girón they could make out the US warships on the horizon. In the event, the ships never joined battle, but they were close enough to see their invasion plans go up in smoke. Che played no direct part in engagements with the enemy, though his cheek was grazed by a stray bullet. The invasion had been crushed before it could build up momentum.

Images of defeat. The sinking of the
Houston, one of the troop carriers.
The prisoners were exchanged for
food and medicine.

The *barbudos* had won again, in what was the superpower's first costly defeat. The island lost 161 combatants, compared to the enemy's loss of 107 *gusanos*. In addition, the Cuban army had captured almost 1,200 prisoners, who were subsequently swapped for $52 million in food and medical supplies. In a prelude to the later and much bigger defeat – Vietnam – the US had underestimated the human factor. They had not foreseen that the fervor every Cuban recruit felt for the national cause could make up for inferior firepower. The Bay of Pigs went down in history as a laughable weekend invasion launched against a government which was supported by the majority of the population. In the

A ceremony to honour prize-winning voluntary workers for their "revolutionary effort". Lenin and Martí in the background: a Caribbean partnership.

EL AIRE Y SOL
DE LA LIBERTAD
JOSE MARTÍ

Nostalgia for *La Poderosa II*? A brief regression to an old passion.

THERE IS AN ERROR IN YOUR PROPOSALS. NO WORKERS RESPONSIBLE FOR THE PRODUCTION OF ANY ARTICLE HAVE RIGHTS OVER IT. BAKERS HAVE NO RIGHT TO EXTRA BREAD, AND WORKERS IN THE CEMENT INDUSTRY HAVE NO SPECIAL CLAIM TO BAGS OF CEMENT. IN THE SAME WAY, YOU ARE NOT ENTITLED TO SPECIAL TERMS ON MOTORCYCLES.

Che. Letter to the workers in the Motorcycle Assembly Plant.

★

"Absenteeism and low productivity are the enemies of industrialisation." Che criticises the 'apathy' shown by the workers.

A minister who loathed offices, and preferred having critical debates with factory workers. Photo by Korda.

Referring to Cuban industry, he said "We were left with absolutely no technology."

BEAUTY IS NOT AT ODDS WITH THE
REVOLUTION. TO MAKE AN ARTEFACT
FOR EVERYDAY USE THAT IS UGLY,
WHEN IT SHOULD BE ATTRACTIVE, IS
QUITE UNACCEPTABLE.

Che

At the Czechoslovakian Exhibition in Havana. For Che, quality control was an obsession.

a few pounds and his beard had been trimmed. His hair was a little shorter swept back so that the beret emphasized the 'V' of hair on his forehead. He also had a rather devilish mien. In the end, even Che would end up carrying a briefcase and wearing a raincoat, looking for all the world like a fur-capped Soviet *apparatchik* – although that particular role was one he would never have agreed to take on.

During the trip to Punta del Este, apart from talking with Kennedy's personal emissary, Richard Goodwin, Che also met three presidents. He shared a friendly *maté* with the President of Uruguay, Eduardo Haedo. On August 18th, Che flew to Buenos Aires to meet the Argentinian President, Arturo Frondizi. Frondizi had initially flirted with Peronism and the Left in order to win the election, and both sides now condemned his change in political direction as 'treason'. Although his interview with Che was chiefly designed to win over his critics, Frondizi also saw himself as a mediator with the White House. A day later he met the Brazilian President, Janio Quadros, who awarded him the order of the *Grande Cruz do Sul* (Great Cross of the South).

The last two presidents paid dearly for their conversations with Che. Quadros was overthrown within a week, with the excuse that he had decorated a Communist. As for Frondizi, the Right used the meeting as a pretext for ejecting him from office six months later. Nonetheless, the Punta del Este trip proved a wise political

The Minister tries out the machinery in a textile factory.

Che visited Prague and Moscow in August 1962. The help provided by the socialist countries was fundamental in helping Cuba to free itself from monoculture farming.

A man and his cigar. Photo by Korda.

investment for Cuba in terms of publicizing the international guerrilla struggle. Although Che's speech at the University of Montevideo ended with the police dispersing the students with tear gas, it planted the seeds of an active *Guevarist* movement in the River Plate area, and nurtured dialogue between Havana and the Left.

Once back in Cuba, the Minister returned the economy, which was beginning to weaken. In addition to the curse of geography, the economy was suffering from bad organization, inexperienced personnel, and an excess of what might be best described as revolutionary voluntarism. Although land reform had substantially improved the situation of the peasants, and consumption was rising steadily, the urban middle class wanted more. Between 1960 and 1963, the Ministry of Industry had embarked on a plan for diversifying agriculture, and discouraging monocrop sugar production. As a result, great stretches of cane were uprooted in order to plant cotton or rice. INRA policies contributed to spontaneous diversification, as peasants – having turned into landowners – tried their hand at growing other crops. All the Ministry's resources were drawn on to mobilize more cane-cutters, but the volunteers – for the most part untrained *peones* (farmworkers) – did not have the skills required. This was a shortcoming which would make itself felt in subsequent harvests.

Back in Cuba, Che went off every weekend, machete in hand, keen to be the first in line to chop the cane that would eventually sweeten the samovars of Moscow. These 'days off' tended to be dawn-to-dusk shifts. In early February 1963, Che experimented with a new cane-cutter as part of the campaign to encourage wider mechanization. But Cuba was encountering major difficulties in developing its own technology and – according to Borrego – these particular machines deserved a place in a catalogue of oddities.

The pictures of Che doing voluntary work (see also p. 114 and 140) were central to the imagery of the Cuban state at that time, and they continue to be used in government campaigns. The images started a dialogue about Che's *guerrillero* past, and asserted the continuity of a revolutionary's work in building socialism during times of peace. The change of job did not even require him to change uniforms. As in the Sierra, so in the cane fields: the color was still olive green, as a reminder that this was the same war continued by other means. The photos also fitted perfectly with Che's ideal of the New Socialist. The swelling produced by the cortisone gave him the look of an exploited worker under capitalism. Like every picture of Che, the photos taken when he was doing voluntary work were conceived as anti-capitalist propaganda. However, when Fidel was criticised for using unpaid labor for work that had previously been paid, he deliberately distanced himself from the practice, leaving the Minister to fend for himself.

So far as the industrialization program was concerned, the State was facing a problem of management. The best-qualified specialists had left the country along with the foreign companies that had employed them. This left the Minister with a long struggle against incompetence. Che knew all too well that the machinery imported from Eastern Europe was well below the standard of Japanese and North American products, and that the only equipment the USSR would ship Cuba would be obsolete. Also, to get the machines working required spare parts that could only be bought from Cuba's foreign earnings – in other words, the income from sugarcane.

Che could be severely critical of his own and other people's mistakes. Some years later, on a trip to Egypt, he admitted to Gamal Nasser that the Revolution had made wrong decisions, and that he might have to accept most of the responsibility for them. He summed up the main cause of the problems in a few words: '98 per cent of what we found, we nationalized.'

The development of Cuba's industries, which had been the Minister's great promise, did not fail to come about because of any weakness on Che's part, but because of Cuban powerlessness in respect of matters that were decided in the Kremlin, rather than in Che's – or even Fidel's – office. One of Che's bitterest defeats came when the USSR complemented the US commercial embargo by announcing its own block to Cuba's economic future. Within the overall Soviet system, industrial production had been assigned to Eastern Europe. For Havana this meant a return to an economy based on cutting cane and rolling tobacco. By way of compensation, Moscow guaranteed Cuba's territorial sovereignty.

The deal took place within the framework of the

EVERYTHING FOR THE REVOLUTION, NOTHING, AGAINST THE REVOLUTION. ... THE REVOLUTION ALSO HAS ITS RIGHTS, THE FIRST OF THEM BEING THE RIGHT TO EXIST.

Fidel Castro, An appeal to intellectuals.

Fidel, as seen through Che's camera.

John Kennedy announced the naval blockade on October 22nd 1962, calling for the immediate withdrawal of the Soviet Union's nuclear missiles. While Cuba was preparing to rebuff a new invasion, Moscow unilaterally negotiated an end to the crisis.

Moscow and Havana had agreed on
the installation of nuclear missiles
on the island. Che deplored the
Soviet government's "treachery".

WE THOUGHT YOU WOULD BE
SATISFIED. WE DID EVERYTHING
WE COULD TO PREVENT CUBA FROM
BEING DESTROYED. WE NOTE YOUR
READINESS TO DIE A BEAUTIFUL
DEATH, BUT WE DON'T THINK
IT'S WORTH IT.

Anastas Mikoyan, the Soviet Vice-
Premier, to Che and other senior civil
servants, November 1962.

THERE WAS A VERY CLOSE RIVALRY BETWEEN US;

WHEN WE DISCOVERED THAT CHE WAS SENDING PEOPLE

TO SPY ON US, WE STARTED TO DO THE SAME.

EVERYTHING WAS SO COMPETITIVE. I MUST ADMIT

THAT WHEN THEY TOLD ME HE WAS SUFFERING FROM

AN ASTHMA ATTACK, I WAS PLEASED.

Statement by Rosario Cueto, volunteer harvester.

**Cutting the sugar cane
in Camegüey, 1963.**

The cane-cutting Minister.

theory of nuclear deterrence, according to which the only way to ensure a balance between the superpowers and their spheres of influence was by maintaining matching levels of firepower, i.e. the policy of mutual assured destruction, or 'MAD'. In early June 1962, with the full knowledge of President Dorticós and Che, Fidel accepted the Soviets' offer to install nuclear missiles. This would give Moscow a counter to the US American rocket sites in Turkey, and Havana a deterrent in the event of a second seaborne invasion. Che signed the missile agreement with Khruschev in the Crimea in August, and building work on the bases began soon afterwards. This was no secret to the Pentagon, and was precisely what they wanted since the essence of their deterrence policy was to ensure that spy planes would quickly locate the bases and spread the news. The growing tension between the superpowers – with Cuba once again the pawn – led to what became known as 'The Cuban Missile Crisis'. This international episode marked the end of Che's political innocence. It was now only a matter of time before his disappointment with Moscow would drive him to a more extreme form of radicalism.

On October 22nd 1962, President Kennedy addressed the US people to inform them, with the help of dramatic photos, that he had 'indisputable evidence' of Soviet bases just 90 miles away from the US coast. He duly announced that he would impose a naval blockade on

The family approach to voluntary work; Che with
Aleida and childhood friend, Alberto Granado.

"The only way to
make the Minister
stop was to tell
him that we were
all exhausted." In
spite of all the
effort expended in
the work, the
1963 harvest was
the worst of the
century.

Castro kept out of the debate about financial incentives and the running of the economy.

"We're going to spend five years here and then we'll leave. When we're both five years older, we'll still be able to put together a guerrilla group." Che, to his secretary, Juan José Manresa, when he took over the Ministry.

Raúl Castro and Che visiting the Nikaro nickel mines.

Cuba. The Soviet ships bearing missiles ignored his warning, and continued their voyage to the Caribbean. This was a new and dangerous form of geopolitical poker. While the Russians were working on the island, Che was once again stationed in Pinar del Río, waiting for the 'imminent' invasion that had already been predicted several times during the course of the year. The spectre of the 'Red [nuclear] Button', and of a second Hiroshima, haunted the entire continent. Politics stood still in the face of catastrophe. The people of Cuba prepared for another invasion.

Then, suddenly, caution prevailed. The USSR and US struck a deal. This was not due to any move by Fidel – who in the middle of the crisis asked Moscow to respond to a possible nuclear attack on Cuba with an equivalent counter-attack – nor on the part of Che, who saw the deal as a Soviet betrayal of past promises. On October 24th, without warning, the ships changed course. Without even informing Havana, Khruschev had reached an agreement with Kennedy to dismantle the bases. In exchange, the US agreed to a policy of non-aggression in the Caribbean, and the removal of its missiles in Turkey. The danger was averted. The Cubans, having discovered they were more isolated than they had thought, took to the streets shouting *'Nikita mariquita, lo que se da no se quita'* ('Nikita, you little faggot/ what you've given you can't take back').

With hindsight, Kruschev seems to have acted reasonably in the circumstances, though he could be censured for lack of courtesy. Fidel, who only heard of the superpowers' deal on the radio, was understandably furious. Since then, although Washington has kept its promise not to invade Cuba, it has instead bled it white through the embargo. Che, who bitterly blamed Moscow for its part in the deal, left his command post and returned to his civil servant's in-tray.

Meanwhile, Che's family continued to grow. In May that year his third child had been born – a boy named Camilo in memory of Camilo Cienfuegos. The family had finally bought a house on 37th Street, in the Nuevo Vedado district, a neighborhood of functional houses where a number of other government members lived. But while their two-storey house may have looked quite bourgeois from the outside, inside the impression was different, as they had hardly any furniture.

Che addressing the crowd. He preferred to speak calmly and reflectively rather than encourage an emotional response.

Everyone – except Che – sitting in their place during the second anniversary of the Union of Young Communists. October 20th 1962.

Following the failure of the sugar harvest, Fidel announced that Cuba "will have to give up its dreams of industrialization".

"We have to paint ourselves as black, as workers, and as peasants..." An address to lecturers and students in the University of Havana.

ALMA MATER

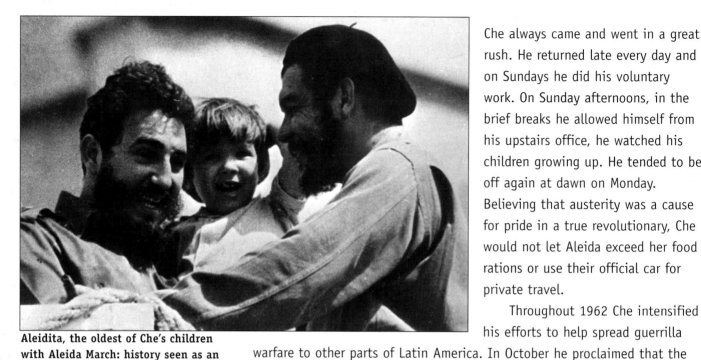

Aleidita, the oldest of Che's children with Aleida March: history seen as an everyday event.

Che always came and went in a great rush. He returned late every day and on Sundays he did his voluntary work. On Sunday afternoons, in the brief breaks he allowed himself from his upstairs office, he watched his children growing up. He tended to be off again at dawn on Monday. Believing that austerity was a cause for pride in a true revolutionary, Che would not let Aleida exceed her food rations or use their official car for private travel.

Throughout 1962 Che intensified his efforts to help spread guerrilla warfare to other parts of Latin America. In October he proclaimed that the Andean mountain range was 'destined to be the Sierra Maestra of the Americas'. The statement reflected Che's character and way of thinking, while the ideas reflected Fidel's foreign policies. Yet although the logic was in keeping with 1960s' ideology, it was not part of the Soviet government's plans.

Che's first son, Camilo, on his first birthday. The family celebrated with the traditional white cake, and an ample stock of Coca Cola.

All of Che's associates, including Castro, have pointed out the importance Che gave to the idea of establishing an armed vanguard in his own country. He talked in terms of inspiring revolutionary *foquismo* (small nuclei of guerrillas). Once again, the possibility of Cuba encouraging armed struggle on the Latin American continent did not coincide with the Soviet

script, which said that every effort should be made to maintain the agreements for 'peaceful coexistence'. Latin America fell into the US sphere of influence, and provided the USSR could maintain its network of local (and extremely docile) Communist parties in the region, it was content to let matters rest. Havana on the other hand knew that in the longer term its only chance of surviving would come as a result of the ideological conquest of Latin America, combined with a strong, clear, continental strategy that would be in tune with the tradition of combative idealism.

For Che, 1963 brought reminders of close emotional ties to his Argentinian past. His third daughter (the fourth child) was born on June 14th, the same date as his own birthday. She was named Celia after his mother, who on her own road to political radicalism spent several months in jail for spreading pro-Cuban propaganda. Her *Guevarist* activism was his mother's way of staying close to her son. In September, the plan for an Argentinian *foco*, or 'pilot' guerrrrilla group, was finally set in motion. It was under Che's control, and led by Jorge Masetti, who set off with a handful of fighters to the northern province of Salta, near the Bolivian border. By April 1964, the Argentinian intelligence forces had liquidated the entire group.

Meanwhile in Cuba, Che was beginning to lose the battle over the economy. The wrangling seemed to come to an end in 1964, when he lost control of the Ministry for the Sugar Industry – the most powerful post in the cabinet. But it was an honorable defeat, and the portfolio ended up in the hands of Che's trusted assistant, Orlando Borrego. In the economic sphere, Havana entered wholeheartedly into an era of pragmatic compliance with Moscow's demands, even though it meant abandoning its previous aspirations of industrialization and agricultural diversification.

By this time, Che had to be on guard not only against the Soviets, who disliked his influence on Cuban foreign policy, but also against the pro-Soviet wing of the government who played up his reputation as a Maoist, a Trotskyite, and a dissident – true to some extent. At this point though, Che's disagreements were not directed against Fidel. But clearly nothing would offend his intelligence more than ending up as a mere agent for the Cuban Revolution. He would prefer to give up his power entirely than to renounce the 'ideal of human perfection' that Borrego had recognized in him. As in 1954, he began to feel like a stranger in Cuba. That panacea, the open road, began to tempt him again. Taking the step that would lead to him becoming a myth, Che turned his back on the safe haven.

EVEN CHE COULD NOT ALWAYS LIVE UP TO BEING CHE. SOMETIMES HE GOT TIRED, TOO, AND RETURNED HOME EXHAUSTED, JUST WANTING TO BE ALONE WITH HIS CHILDREN.

Haydee Santamaría, the heroine of the attack on the Moncada.

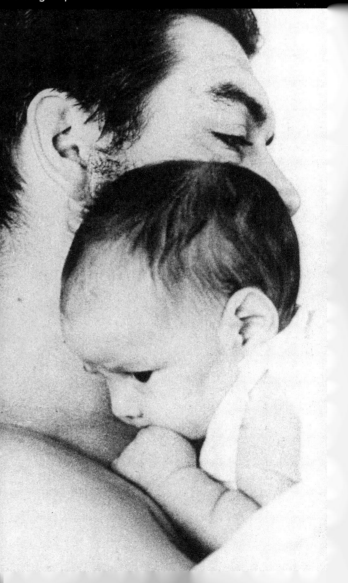

ON THE ROAD AGAIN

On November 4th 1964, Che set out on a diplomatic mission that began in Moscow and lasted for three months. Everything had changed in the four years since he had first walked into the Red Square. Khruschev had been replaced by the more conservative Leonid Brezhnev. More importantly, Che now saw Cuba's relations with Moscow in a much more critical light. The purpose of the visit was to confirm Cuba's allegiances in the Sino–Soviet dispute, and to settle the details of the first – and only – meeting of Latin American Communist Parties, which was to take place in Havana.

Che arrived in New York on December 11th to represent Cuba at the United Nations. He made an explosive début. Speaking with all the directness of a political pamphleteer, he attacked the curators of US imperialism in Latin America, demanding an end to the blockade and the removal of the US base at Guantánamo – the source of constant sabotage attempts. He also paid tribute to the Congo leader, Patrice Lumumba, who had been assassinated on January 17th 1961. By this time, African struggles for independence and liberation were eagerly followed in Havana, since they provided a potential battleground for 'proletarian internationalism'. When Che spoke, his clothes, appearance and informal manner stood as a condemnation of everything around him, underlining the fact that, at heart, the UN was a sham.

A week later, Che was in Algeria to meet the independence leader, Ahmed Ben Bella. This was the beginning of an African tour that took in Tanzania, Egypt, Mali, Ghana, and Dahomey (now Benin). The trip was also a preparation for an incursion into the former Belgian

BY THIS TIME (1964) CHE HAD DEVELOPED A PRECISE AND WELL-DEFINED ANALYSIS OF

THE INTERNAL WORKINGS OF THE SOCIALIST COUNTRIES. IN HIS VIEW, THE REASON THEY

WERE LOSING THE RACE AGAINST THE WEST WAS NOT BECAUSE THEY WERE FOLLOWING

MARXIST-LENINISM AXIOMS, BUT THAT THEY WERE BETRAYING OR DISCARDING THEM.

In 1960, Che had been received with honor. Four years later, all that he and the Soviets had left was their mutual distrust

TODAY OUR EYES ARE FREE TO SEE
WHAT OUR PREVIOUS STATUS, AS
COLONIAL SLAVES, PREVENTED US
FROM SEEING: BEHIND ITS
ATTRACTIVE FAÇADE, "WESTERN
CIVILIZATION" HIDES A PACK OF
HYENAS AND JACKALS.

Che, addressing the United Nations

Ordinary uniform for Che in a sea of suits.
United Nations, December 1964.

Che added, with heavy irony, "I trust that the representative for
Nicaragua has not picked up any trace of an American accent in my
speech. Now that would be dangerous."

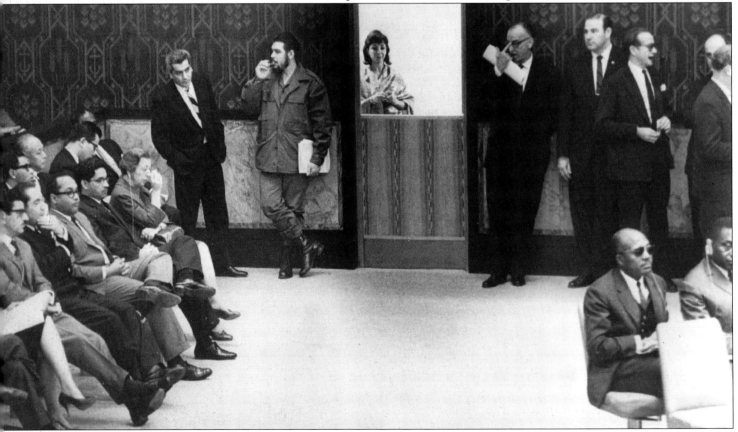

"We have maintained that peaceful coexistence between countries does not admit the coexistence of the exploited and the exploiters, or of the oppressors and the oppressed." A warning shot directed at the USSR.

Arriving in New York, December 9th 1964.

Congo (now Democratic Republic of Congo). When Che sought the opinion of several leaders about his plans to support African insurgents, he received only gloomy forecasts. Nasser was especially pessimistic, warning that in the African context there was a danger of any white leader being identified as a 'Tarzan' figure.

Half-way through the tour, Che suddenly left to make a rather bizarre visit to Beijing. Relations between the Chinese and the Soviets were extremely tense at this time. Although officially non-aligned, Cuba – as a pawn in the superpowers' game – took an increasingly partisan stand on Moscow's side. The result was that Che was forced to provide explanations for a position he personally did not share, but for which he would be held responsible. This time Mao did not even say hello to him.

The commercial treaty that sealed Cuba's economic dependence was signed in Moscow in mid-February, in Che's absence. The agreement could be seen as the beginning of the end of any hopes for industrialization and agricultural diversification for which his Ministry had fought so hard. Sugar exports to the USSR were to be increased, which meant that Cuba would return to its one-crop economy. Although Soviet aid would be greatly increased, one area of conflict still dogged the two countries' relations. This was Cuba's covert foreign policy, which was wrapped up in the phrase 'proletarian internationalism'. It was also an area under Che's control.

When Che returned to Algeria on February 24th, he was told that Aleida had given birth to a son named Ernesto after him. This, his last child, was the second to be born while he was away from home. The Conference of Afro-Asian Solidarity, then taking place in Algeria,

★

THE SOCIALIST COUNTRIES ARE UNDER A MORAL OBLIGATION TO END THEIR TACIT COMPLICITY WITH THE EXPLOITATIVE COUNTRIES OF THE WEST... THE QUESTION OF [SEEKING] LIBERATION FROM AN OPPRESSIVE POLITICAL POWER BY FORCE OF ARMS MUST BE RESOLVED IN ACCORDANCE WITH THE RULES OF THE INTERNATIONAL PROLETARIAT.

Che. Speech given in Algiers, 27 February 1965.

justified his sacrifice. The problems of the Third World were to be debated, while behind the scenes aid was being put together to support various African liberation struggles. Che, well aware that he had failed to win the power struggle in Cuba, was clear and detached. He delivered his famous speech denouncing the socialist bloc as a form of secondary imperialism that extorted the countries it protected: 'If we set up this kind of relationship between the two groups of countries, then we should at least agree that the socialist countries are, to a certain extent, accomplices in imperial exploitation... The socialist states have a moral duty to end their tacit complicity with the exploiting countries of the West.' At the same time Che made a declaration of faith in guerrilla internationalism, proposing one 'grand, compact bloc' comprised of nations in the process of liberation, that should be armed and freely assisted by those socialist countries with weapon-producing capacity. By expressing his demands in this way, Che was sending a challenge to his supporters in Havana. The question was, would Fidel tolerate having a member of his government make public criticisms of the Soviet Union? As events turned out, the Algiers speech marked the point of no return for *Realpolitik*.

When Che returned to Cuba on March 15th, he was hardly given a moment to greet his wife at the airport – there was a court waiting for him behind closed doors. Fidel – who was accompanied either by President Dorticós or by Raúl Castro, according to which source one believes – locked himself away with Che for two days and nights to demand an explanation for his Algiers speech. Ministry of Industry matters could have been no more than a footnote to that meeting. The Castro brothers were in

agreement: Che would have to leave the government. By this time Che had already decided to leave Cuba. In the year when the definitive biographies of Che were published every new reading had to take that meeting into account, and was obliged to find some explanation. This one encounter between Castro and Che, more than anything else, is what keeps historians of Cuba awake at night, since it determines the nautre of their separation. It is also precisely the moment that reveals each author's ideological stance. Jon Lee Anderson's pro-government line is little given to emphasizing the discrepancies at the heart of the Cuban government, and maintains that Fidel's criticisms were strictly related to matters of style. However even Anderson admits that since the internal pressure directed against the 'Maoist' was becoming unbearable, Fidel had 'suggested' to Che that he should leave Cuba to provide support for the guerrilla group that he had already spent some time in training. The

With President Nasser. Cuba seeks an anti-imperialist front with Egypt, Algeria and Tanzania.

French author, Jean Cormier, who openly sympathizes with Castro, argued that 'Che couldn't stay in Cuba and didn't want to', knowing that 'he had become a burden for Fidel, now that he was no longer popular with Moscow'. The Mexican writer, Jorge Castañeda, attributes the decision to a bitter dispute with Fidel and in particular with Raúl Castro, the most pro-Soviet figure. Finally, Che's biographer Paco Taibo tried to resolve the enigma by looking at the puzzle from a new angle, suggesting that the question of why Che left Cuba can only be answered with another question: why had he stayed so long? One of many reasons why there has not been a Cuban biography of Che is precisely because it would have to explain this point.

Che's decision to take to the road again had Fidel's support. Castro knew that Cuban independence depended on expanding its sphere of influence. For Che, this represented a chance to fight in 'the hottest spot in the world'. The consistency between Che's writings and his life was such that together they

Wherever he goes, Che finds signs of solidarity with Cuba.

Back in Havana, 15th March 1965. Che has to account for his statements in Algeria.

constituted a single work. Even after the utopian dream had collapsed, as a result of 'unpredicted errors' stemming from Che's paradoxical nature – the direct correspondence between his actions and his ideas continued to the end.

Che's diary notes from the Congo were stored away for almost 30 years. They finally came to light in 1990, when fragments were introduced into a narrative by Paco Taibo. The manuscripts have never been published in full, and it is difficult to gain access to them. No one was more critical of the Congo experience than its leader. For Che, the years 1965–6 in all their alarming detail were considered a period of nomadic re-initiation, during which the process of self-questioning and personal discovery landed him in a metaphysical desert. He was setting out again to revive his own myth. But before leaving he wanted to transform himself by returning to anonymity, and discarding the trappings of a government minister, founding member and first ideologue of the Revolution.

May Day 1963, with Raúl and Fidel Castro. Two years later, the triumvirate was less united. Che decided to leave in search of his "African Vietnam".

Now came the time for farewells. He asked a secretary to return an anthology of poems to Fernández Retamar. This was how Retamar came to realize that Che had transcribed one of the poems, Pablo Neruda's 'Farewell'. Che sent his mother an ambiguously-worded letter; reading between the lines, she was able to discern that he had suffered a political defeat. He told her that he was leaving for the Oriente region to help with the harvest, but that once

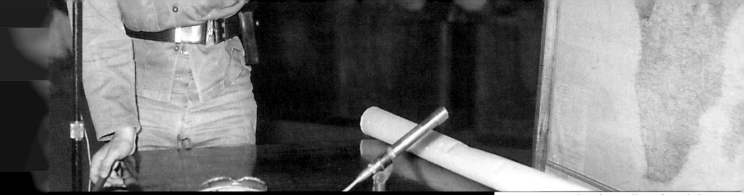

that was over he had been thinking of starting a business – presumably state-owned – with his friend, Alberto Granado. Celia was alarmed that he had fallen from favor. She had never got on very well with Fidel, and when she tried to make contact with her son through Aleida she was told that it would not be possible. Aleida could not even reassure her by saying that he was undergoing military training in advance of his mission to the Congo. The lack of communication between Celia and her son took on a funereal aspect. Because of her terminal illness, the mother who had inspired him returned to hospital for the last time. She sent him a final letter full of concern, where she counseled him to offer his economic advice to the leaders of Ghana and Algeria. She would not have the opportunity to speak to her son again. Her letter crossed with another from Che, but she died before it arrived.

Che's letter to his family announcing his departure included a quotation from Cervantes, and another from the Nicaraguan poet, Rubén Darío: 'Dear folks, Once again I can feel Rocinante's ribs beneath my heels; I'm returning to the road, with my shield on my arm.' Che heard of Celia's death when he was in the Congo. From that moment on, he lived an undercover existence. His children would not speak with their father again.

The expression of Che's greatest sadness may have been reserved for

MY CARAVAN WILL BE RUNNING ON TWO FEET AGAIN, AND THERE'LL BE NO LIMIT TO MY DREAMS. UNTIL THE BULLETS DECIDE THINGS FOR ME, AT LEAST... I'LL BE EXPECTING YOU, YOU SEDENTARY GYPSY, WHEN THE DUST HAS SETTLED.

Dedication in a book sent to Alberto Granado

his famous farewell message to Fidel, possibly the best piece he ever wrote. It was a fervent declaration of friendship that included an emotional account of his revolutionary development. But it was also a confession that, in any event, Fidel would not be able to return – the next-to-last favor the Argentinian could contribute to Castro's political hand. 'At this moment I'm recalling many things: such as when I met you at María Antonia's house, when you suggested I should join you, and all the pressure to get everything ready. One day they came round asking who to notify if we were killed, and suddenly it came home to us that it was a real possibility. Later on we saw for ourselves that it was true, that in a revolution (if it's a real one) you either win or you die... I take this opportunity to say, once more, that I free Cuba from any responsibility, except for the example it gave to me. If I meet my final hour under foreign skies, my last thoughts will be of this people, and especially of you... Until victory always. Fatherland or death! I embrace you with all revolutionary fervor: Che'.

The letter was tinged with submissiveness. Che was recognizing Fidel as his mentor, and confessing his disciple's veneration. As a token of his gratitude, he renounced his position and his military rank, his Cuban citizenship... everything he had built: a family, a place in the revolution, the love of the people. He no longer had a name. He was ready for his last journey.

It is revealing that, for the first time in ten years, Che had to discard his battle dress in order to embark on another war. To slip away without

ABOVE ALL, [YOU MUST] ALWAYS BE READY TO FEEL, TO THE DEPTH OF YOUR BEING, ANY INJUSTICE COMMITTED AGAINST ANY PERSON, ANYWHERE IN THE WORLD. THAT IS THE BEST OF ALL REVOLUTIONARY QUALITIES.

Papá

The last family portrait. Che with his two sons, Camilo and Ernestito, the baby. Aleidita, the oldest, and Celia, with their mother. March 1965.

attracting attention, he disguised himself as a capitalist. A haircut, a shave and an uncomfortable prosthesis in his mouth made him into an unconvincing image of the one thing he could never be – a bourgeois man on a business trip. The disguise was the transition he needed to 'de-Cubanize' himself. In the photos, he bears a striking resemblance to Orson Welles in 'Citizen Kane': 'to deceive my enemy, I will become as my enemy'.

In the meantime, the international press was spreading absurd rumors. Some of them were supplied by the pro-Soviet 'old guard' in Havana, who variously portrayed Che as Fidel's ghost, his Trotsky or his China-loving dissident. International news agencies had Che interned in a psychiatric ward in Mexico, jailed in a Havana gulag after a bitter battle with Fidel, and dead in Santo Domingo. Meanwhile, the mysterious 'Ramón Benítez' was playing hide-and-seek with the world's intelligence agencies. After a detour that lasted 17 days, he finally reached Tanzania.

Recent interpretations suggest that Fidel advised Che to go to the Congo in order to dissuade him from returning to the struggle in Latin America. There is no doubt that the failure of the *foco* led by Masetti in Argentina had indicated to Che that the moment was not yet ripe for insurrection in that country. On the other hand, according to the logic of proletarian internationalism – which considered that wherever people were oppressed was a good place to fight US imperialism – the journey to Africa made sense. Castro had also come to believe that success in the Congo might just convince Moscow to modify its foreign policy, and take a roundabout route to the Andes by way of Africa. Even so, while Fidel gave his full backing to Che's departure to the Congo, there were associated political risks. In the words of Ulíses Estrada, Che's bodyguard, 'If Che died in the Congo, it would cause an international scandal; if Che died in Bolivia, he would be a martyr.'

On April 14th 1965 Che was back in Tanzania. The frontier with the Congo was the agreed meeting point for all of the continent's revolutionary leaders. It seemed at the time that the followers of the murdered Congo leader, Patrice Lumumba, would be returning to the armed struggle. The country was now a quasi-colony presided over by Moise Tshombé, and supported by Belgium and the US. From the standpoint of the guerrillas, the main problem was that the campaign was divided in two fronts. One, operating in the west, was led by one of Lumumba's former ministers, Pierre Mulele. The other front, that of the Committee of National Liberation (CLN) in the north and east of the country, was led by a number of leaders, including Laurent Kabila

TEN YEARS AGO, I WROTE YOU ANOTHER FAREWELL LETTER... THIS MAY BE THE LAST ONE. NOT BECAUSE I WANT IT TO BE, BUT BECAUSE IT FALLS WITHIN THE LOGICAL CALCULATION OF PROBABILITIES...

Che. Letter of farewell to his parents.

The *guerrillero* mock
the intelligenc
services by assumin
the outwar
appearance of
middle-class travele
on a business trip
Che left Cuba o
April 1st 1965

ly take power some 30 years later). Although the
han fully committed to the cause, they were kept well
and Chinese arms. Moscow supplied the CLN, and
ele.

disillusioned with the leaders of the revolution. In the
kept in the Congo, *Pasajes de la guerra revolucionaria*
Revolutionary War') he referred to them pejoratively in
ighters' who enjoyed a comfortable hotel lifestyle, and
ed in receiving 'military training in Cuba and monetary
ed that the Congolese should do their training *in situ*,
cording to the Cuban Ambassador in Tanzania, Pablo
eally wanted to do was to leave the Congo, not go back
instructors who made up the first contingent were later
00.

or Dreke recalled in his memoirs a series of bizarre
Congolese that reveal the contrast between the African
an Revolution. 'We had preconceived ideas that didn't
eep in a hammock because you'd have three snakes
ou.' Similarly, 'until we showed them some photos, they
ack. There was widespread illiteracy, there were no
ad no idea who Che was'. For them he was just *Muganga*
Swahili nickname he had taken shortly after arriving.
tra, Che found time to heal sick peasants: time was the

THIS ISN'T YOUR MOTHER SPEAKING, IT'S AN

ELDERLY LADY WHO HOPES TO SEE THE

WHOLE WORLD CONVERTED TO SOCIALISM. IF,

FOR WHATEVER REASON, SOME OF THE DOORS

THAT WERE OPEN TO YOU IN CUBA HAVE

BEEN CLOSED, IN ALGERIA THERE'S A

CERTAIN MR BEN BELLA WHO WOULD BE

GRATEFUL IF YOU COULD SORT OUT THE

ECONOMY THERE... YES, IT DOES SEEM AS IF

YOU'LL ALWAYS BE A FOREIGNER. IT SEEMS

TO BE YOUR FINAL DESTINY.

Letter from Celia de la Serna, April 1965.

only thing that wasn't in short supply.

In spite of the culture clash, Cuban involvement grew. They were surprised by the animist beliefs of the rebels, and the use they made of *dawas* (medicine), and viewed with some disdain the rituals local people carried out to protect themselves before going into battle. Above all, Che scorned the laziness of the Congolese guerrilla fighters, who hired peasants as carriers. His diary records their 'slothfulness in not going to the base to get food... If they were given something to carry, they'd say *Mimi apana motocari* ('I'm not a truck') or *Mimi apana cubana* ('I'm not a Cuban'). They frequently went on strike: 'No food, no work.'

There were isolated, small-scale skirmishes, the most notable being the assault on Fort Bendera, where four Cubans died. The Cuban involvement turned into an endless wait, led by a Che who had to 'beg for permission' to leave the base with his troops. What he found most frustrating was that he could not take part in the engagements, since he was expected to take care of himself ('my precious person') by staying to the rear, as his notoriety would alert the counter-revolutionaries. This was stalemate, rather than action, giving him the feeling that he was 'still here on a scholarship.'

Che came to acknowledge that they were acting out a parody of a war. When he visited the town of Mbolo the local combatants organized a parade – he called it a 'show' – to be reviewed by one of the leaders. General Maulana appeared wearing extraordinary headgear: a leopard-skin motorcycle helmet: 'The absurdity reached Chaplinesque proportions. It was as if I was standing there, bored and hungry, watching a bad comedy, while

From an Epic to a Novel

The historian would like to be able to call upon Che's own voice. There is no way of escaping that narrative style, that son-of-a-bitch sincerity, that caustic sense of humor, but... the hypothetical "Prague Notebooks", assuming they exist, have not been made public.

Paco Taibo II. Ernesto Guevara,
Also Known As Che.

Top floor, Cuban Embassy, Tanzania.

The next three months were a time for physical and spiritual convalescence. Che again went over the letter which Fidel had made public in Havana. Once he had formally announced the division between them – and he had already had been trying to put his thoughts into words – there would be no going back. Dar es Salaam marked the beginning of a form of circular banishment. He was not prepared to consider returning to Cuba until he had fulfilled his promise of achieving a triumph for the guerrillas. By this time he was no longer a Cuban citizen. He was a revolutionary without a homeland.

Meanwhile, Fidel was behaving like a slightly guilty friend, sending Che repeated messages to say that he would welcome his return. Aleida traveled to Dar es Salaam to persuade Che that his family was waiting for him, and Ambassador Ribalta saw them embrace, laugh and talk about the children. But Che received messages from Cuban intelligence that would require him to continue his travels. Guevara Lynch's widow, Ana María Erra, believes that Che's decision to continue the armed struggle was influenced by his age and his asthma: 'Ernesto knew he had abused bronchial dilators, and that his heart was no longer very strong. He also knew he was not a young man any more, and that if he wanted to fight again this would be his last opportunity.'

Che took advantage of this time to correct the chapter about the Congo in his *Pasajes de la guerra revolucionaria*. Shutting the door, he took a picture of himself with an automatic camera. That one image expresses the entire existential theme of the 20th century. The photographic self-portrait, that symptom *par excellence* of modernity, was the last resort of the traveler who no longer believed in any message other than the mask that is his own face; his body is frozen

"He [sic] has decided to subject himself to strict discipline. He will carry out certain acts, crossing the road at predetermined corners, touching a particular tree or railing, so that the future will be as irrevocable as the past."

Jorge Luis Borges. May 20th 1928.

in a fragment of time: a portrait of the artist as a lost character. The experience in the Congo, and above all his present impasse, called for a change. The triumphant leading character had lost; the hero had become an anti-hero. He did not know where to go. He wrote in his diary: 'Who was I?' He wanted to go home.

Dar es Salaam, and afterwards Prague, were the opposite of Guatemala and Mexico. In 1955 Che had the opportunity to choose from a range of options; in 1966 the future was closing off before him. This period, one of the most intense and unusual of his life, revealed a mature man who was weighing his certainties against his never-admitted doubts. Che was caught in a vicious cycle of uncertainty. The Congo, which had been his first revolutionary failure, had prompted his life-story to jump from one genre to another: his life was no longer an epic of the Cuban people, but a novel about a foreigner who had come to a dead end. His final decision evoked the inner demons of Captain Ahab, no longer hunting for the white whale itself so much as hunting for the whiteness of the whale.

Early in March, Che traveled incognito to Prague. He spent three and half months there, hiding out in a one-room apartment, guarded by Juan Carretero and Ulises Estrada. Both these men had 'been present' on the guerrilla operation led by Masetti; it had been coordinated from Bolivia, which indicated that Cuba still had valuable human resources there. Although there had been no spontaneous uprising, in 1965 the brothers Guido 'Inti' and Roberto 'Coco' Peredo, Bolivian communists allied to Havana, had proposed to Che that they should form a *foco* in their country. Those close to Che, including Fidel, had managed to convince him that it was still too early to launch the struggle in Argentina. With that option discarded, Bolivia was the next best choice. Because it was at the center of the continent, the presence of a guerrilla group could spread from there to the neighboring countries. However, with hindsight, it is clear that precedence was given to geographical advantages over an unfavorable political situation.

In Prague Che spent his days studying chess, and listening to music by Miriam Makeba and the Beatles. Che didn't like rock music at first but later admitted that it had a certain charm.

Fearful that he might be discovered, Che grew nervous when one of his companions called him *Comandante* and forgot to use his cover name, Ramón. At first his bodyguard Estrada cleaned the apartment, but Che quickly suggested that they should both do it. They only went out at night, to eat on the edge of town. Since Estrada was the only black man in the city, he became such an exotic figure that Che asked for him to be replaced.

At some stage during those months in Prague Che probably met with Tamara Bunke, who had served as his translator during his visit to East Germany. Since then the young German-Argentinian woman, whose cover name was Tania, had carried out work as a secret agent. After infiltrating the Bolivian government, she eventually ended up joining Che in the countryside.

After holding out for a long time, Che finally agreed to return to Cuba incognito. He did not go to his house, nor would he ever see his children again, except in disguise. He began training again, hiding away in Pinar del Río to get his body back into shape for war. The impasse had come to an end.

Prague, for Che, provided the setting for an interminable period of waiting, mixed with reading, chess, and dreams of returning to the fight in Argentina.

- WHERE ARE YOU NOW, SIR KNIGHT, THE

PUREST KNIGHT, THE BEST KNIGHT?

- LIGHTING THE *GUERRILLERO*'S TORCH, LADY,

IN THE DARK.

Mirta Aguirre. "A song for Che, in the old style."

THE LONELINESS
OF THE GUERRILLERO

Very few people knew that Che was in Cuba. One of them was his friend Orlando Borrego, Minister of the Sugar Industry, who offered to accompany him to Bolivia. Che promised to save a place for him. One souvenir that survived from those evenings is a photo that Borrego has in his office and will not give up for anything. It shows Che with short hair and no beard, looking handsome and fit. The two men are sitting in adjacent armchairs. His friend sets up the camera and the time-lapse mechanism, and runs to sit down next to Che. At the very moment the camera goes off, the chair falls over and they both struggle to hold back their laughter. It was to be Che's last-recorded smile.

The exercise régime helped Che's body grow stronger but according to Borrego, it was a tougher job to keep his spirits up. Che began his last round of written farewells, all of which eventually passed into the care of the Cuban state. In June 1997, the newspaper *Juventud Rebelde* published a note addressed to Carlos Rafael Rodriguez, an orthodox Communist with whom Che had sharply disagreed on matters to do with economics: 'Carlos, from the stirrups of Rocinante I come to attention and salute you. Other suns will shine on my theories and will suit me well enough, but I sense that you'll feel something is missing when there is no-one left to disagree with. I'll bid you goodbye as always: Yes, I'm right, yes, we can win a war

Fidel and one of Che's fake passports. In this one, Che presented himself as Adolfo Mena.

Well-disguised: self-portrait taken with an automatic camera in the Hotel Copacabana on his first day in La Paz, November 3rd 1966.

You have to take the war to wherever the enemy takes it: to their houses, the places they go to relax... [and] you have to do it to the limit. You've got to deny them even a moment's peace, a minute's rest when away from his barracks, and even when inside them; [you have to] attack wherever you can find them, make them feel like a wild animal, hounded wherever it goes.

Che, Make One, Two, Three Vietnams.

"Ramón" *en route* from La Paz to Ñancahuazú, November 2nd 1966. On the next day, Che began his diary in a notebook he bought during a stop-over in Frankfurt.

A false passport in the name of Ramón Benítez, Uruguayan businessman. Che had used the same identity before, in Tanzania and Prague.

like this one (and we will). An embrace from Che.'

Che chose the people who would follow him: Harry Villegas, dubbed 'Pombo' in the Congo; Carlos Coello, alias 'Tuma'; and Benigno. Rebels from the Sierra and *compañeros* from the Ministry, they all belonged to the entourage known as 'Che's men'. The 20 volunteers who joined up were introduced to a man in glasses who looked like a business traveler. They would only learn his identity at the end of the meeting.

Disguised with a prosthesis in his mouth to alter its shape, and a carefully plucked bald spot, Che's reincarnation had the cruelty of a funeral prank. It was his second impossible metamorphosis: he would never live to go bald or grow old. In a supremely stoical act, he had his children brought to the ranch and tried out his disguise several times in front of them. After introducing himself as 'Ramón', Che let his children kiss him without a word. His ability to renounce everything could be seen everywhere in these tragi-comic scenes, from his control over his emotions to his silence.

At his last supper with Che, Castro held forth for hours in an attempt to keep the farewell gathering alive. They were due to leave for the airport at dawn. Standing at a discreet distance from the table – a few guests were left – Castro waited for the aeroplane to cross the sky. Che was flying off to war.

We know how hard Che had worked to put in place the *foco* led by Masetti in 1963. Preparations for the Bolivian guerrilla action reminded him of the defeat of the Salta group, in north-west Argentina, and of his dreams to carry the revolution to his own country. Those dreams were wrapped up in a play of words that by this point he could not recall without bitterness. The *nom de guerre* Masetti had chosen was *Comandante* Segundo, after Don Segundo Sombra, a famous *gaucho* from Argentinian literature. But the person who would actually be in charge, and would be joining the group as the rebellion advanced, was called 'Martín Fierro', another equally famous gaucho, whose identity may be imagined. In January 1955, Che had given Hilda Gadea a copy of the Argentinian national poem of that name. It contained his eloquent dedication: 'So that on the day of my departure you hold on to my underlying ambition for new horizons, and my combative fatalism.' In the end, the dream of the revolutionary – to be at one with his homeland – would only be granted to his myth.

Two years after the Masetti guerrilla group had been crushed, its urban support network remained active, and helped to coordinate the Bolivian

THINGS ARE LOOKING GOOD IN THIS OUT-OF-THE-WAY PLACE, AND EVERYTHING SUGGESTS THAT WE'LL BE ABLE TO STAY FOR AS LONG AS WE WANT. THE PLANS ARE: WAIT FOR THE OTHERS, INCREASE THE NUMBER OF BOLIVIANS TO AT LEAST 20, AND START OPERATIONS.

*Che, Bolivian Diary,
assessment reached in November 1966*

The house the guerrillas purchased in Ñancahuazú, which was the only one in the area with a zinc roof. Che pointed out a neighbor who suspected them of refining cocaine

"Ramón" will never have another chance to wear his beret or his major's star in Bolivia. The peaked cap hides his near bald patch

An equestrian snap. The mules were purchased from 'Loro' Vázquez Viaña, a Bolivian combatant.
6th January 1967.

foco. In 1966 there was no spontaneous armed uprising in Bolivia. The dictatorship of General René Barrientos was based on a pact between the military and the peasants (who had been guaranteed benefits from the 1952 land reform). In Bolivia, one of the continent's most politicized countries, protest was embodied in the tin miners, who though few in number were strong in terms of their political power.

Throughout Latin America, the readiness of local Communist Parties to follow Moscow's orders to the letter had led to the emergence of a range of Maoist and Trotskyite splinter groups. The Secretary-General of the Bolivian Communist Party, Mario Monje, had played a tangential role in supporting Masetti. Now Cuba was requiring a much greater commitment: Monje was asked, not just to provide a few fighters, but to incorporate the Party into the armed struggle. Drawing on all of his revolutionary aura, Che threatened both the Secretary-General and the unity of his Party, which faced the danger of losing its youth wing. Che compelled him to decide who to betray. It took Monje less than a minute to make up his mind.

On November 3rd 1966, 'Adolfo

December 31st December 1966.
A late visit from Mario Monje, General Secretary of the Bolivian Communist Party. Monje's refusal to support the guerrilla force proved a decisive factor in its eventual failure.

'Tania' (Tamara Bunke), taking a photograph and being photographed. The habit of recording the daily routine of guerrilla life would prove to be fatal.

Mena', a Uruguayan official working for the Organization of American States arrived in La Paz. In his room in the Copacabana Hotel, Che took his own picture with the timer. He seems to be remote from his own image, at the center of a triple frame: a mirror, a wooden door and the border of the photo itself: he has become someone else.

It transpired that Havana had only sent 27 recruits: 15 Cubans and 12 Bolivians. To provide support in the cities, they brought in the Argentinian, Ciro Bustos, a former member of the Segundo project in Salta, who would connect them to the Buenos Aires underground. The French intellectual Régis Debray would be responsible for communicating between the *foco*, Cuba and activists in Europe. The group had bought a house in the south-east of Bolivia, in Ñancahuazú. The only people living in the town were the local police and a few peasants. Che had already renounced his two previous homelands, and the Bolivian bush would add to his sense of double exile, and to his deadly paradox, which was that while he fought to end frontiers, Che himself had no roots, and lacked what would normally be thought of as a sense of belonging. In strongly nationalist Bolivia, indigenous identity retained a deep political meaning. Resistance to power, only expressed by the subtle weapons of the weak, was rooted in the local languages Quechua and Aymara. In Bolivia the universalist dream was shattered: Che was seen there as a foreigner.

Although Castro maintained that a legion of volunteers had been intercepted by Monje, this was not the case. The effect of the Party's sabotage was to deepen Che's isolation, and to cut off contact with those who wished to join him. Although communist media around the world

"Tania" – Tamara Bunke, the daughter of a German family – was born in Argentina. The family moved to East Berlin, where she met Che in 1960.

AFTER SHE CARRIED OUT TASKS AS A SPY FOR THE REVOLUTIONARY GOVERNMENT IN CUBA, IN MARCH 1964 CHE GAVE TANIA THE MISSION OF LIVING IN BOLIVIA, WHERE SHE MANAGED TO INFILTRATE THE GOVERNMENT. BUT SHE DREAMED OF FIGHTING ON THE FRONT LINE, AND WAS EVENTUALLY ADMITTED INTO THE GUERRILLA GROUP'S REARGUARD. "TANIA WAS A VERY DIFFICULT WOMAN, WHO WAS NEVER VERY READY TO FOLLOW ORDERS. SHE HAD HER OWN IDEAS ABOUT EVERYTHING, AND LOVED TO ARGUE. SHE WAS VERY STRONG, AND I LOVED HER."

Statement by Ulises Estrada

condemned Che's 'adventurism', when he recruited rebels he continued to employ a relaxed standard of security. The Bolivians were untrained, weapons were scarce, and means of communication were poor.

On November 7th 1966, Che began his diary in a bright red notebook. He set up the *foco*'s base near to the house in Ñancahuazú, and stored arms, food and medicine there. The *guerrilleros* took classes in Quechua. On 1st February the group headed out to reconnoiter the terrain. Communications failed that month, when the radio broke down. Havana found out about this shortly afterwards, but never sent a replacement. It appeared that the guerrilla group in the mountains had been born, and would die, in isolation. Che was forced to rely on his own judgement, with little reference to outside reality.

In early March, three of the Bolivian rebels escaped and betrayed the cause by revealing information about the operation and the identity of its commander. Although the Bolivian government and Washington were increasingly sure that 'Ramón' was Che, they took special care not to disclose their secret to the press. They knew that his name could awaken significant support. The government decreed emergency rule in the area.

With the region surrounded by soldiers, on April 3rd Che took the decision to divide his force in two. He headed a group of 30 men directed south, to Muyupampa. He was joined by Régis Debray and Ciro Bustos. His rearguard, commanded by Juan Vitalo Acuña, nicknamed 'Joaquín', would advance along another route in an attempt to distract the Army, rejoining Che later on. In the meantime, Tania, who had been working in Buenos Aires, returned to Bolivia. Since she was seriously ill with fever she stayed in the rearguard, under Joaquín's orders.

During this time Che's group carried out what would

be their most important actions, by capturing weapons and leaving 18 dead and 20 wounded among the regular troops. Their most effective action was at Iripití on April 11th. These were incursions into tiny towns to make contact with the people and obtain provisions.

In the same week the front page of the newspaper *Granma* published Che's message to the Tricontinental, a meeting of delegates from Asia, Africa and Latin America. 'Our motto is: Create two, three... many Vietnams!' This would be one of his most influential texts. At a moment when political violence was seen as offering the only solution to the struggles of oppressed peoples, Che offered a prescient vision of himself: 'Every drop of blood spilled in a land under whose flag you were not born, is an experience to be applied at a later stage by all those who survive to the liberation struggles of their own country of origin... Wherever death may surprise us, we will welcome it, so long as our battle cry has reached at least one receptive ear...' The publication of this speech was a sign of Castro's firm support for the Bolivian campaign, and his ratification of Che's foreign policy. In short, it represented a slap in the face of the pro-Soviet groups.

On April 20th, luck finally abandoned the insurgents. Debray and Bustos were detained after they had split off from the column to carry out assigned tasks. The event proved to be catastrophic. Suspicions that he had talked would always weigh heavily on Bustos, who without receiving a single blow drew identikit sketches of Che, Benigno and the Peruvian

In the camp, from left to right, Alejandro, Pombo, Urbano, Rolando, Che, Tuma, Arturo and Moro. "We've got a reasonable amount of food for three days; today 'El Ñato' killed a bird with his catapult, so we're about to enter the Age of the Bird."
Che, Bolivian Diary.

For reconnaissance purposes they spent the first months in the Ñancahuazú region taking long walks.

Juan Pablo 'Chino' Chang, a soldier of oriental origin who was deaf and short-sighted (see p. 182). Che noted in his diary that those two losses marked the deepening of the group's isolation because they cut off its links to Cuba and Argentina. Information also provided by Bustos led the Army to the caves near the Ñancahuazú safe house.

President Barrientos, with help from US soldiers and CIA officials, aimed to end the uprising at an early stage by sending in thousands of men. These were no demoralized Batista regulars: starting in May, US counter-insurgency intelligence began training a company of 600 Rangers. These soldiers were strongly nationalistic, and firmly convinced they were fighting an alien and atheistic enemy. The hunt began in July.

Che was in the middle of a wilderness, hemmed into a small territory, and systematically informed against by terrified peasants who had been threatened with harsh treatment at the hands of the Army Rangers. Faced with Debray's insistence on going into battle, Che had told him that on the front line ten urban intellectuals would be worth less than a single shepherd. He had still failed to recruit a single peasant. At the same time, there was a genuine outbreak of conflict in the tin mines, to the point that in May the region's miners seized the mineral deposits in support of the *foco*, and declared them to be on 'liberated territory'. Barrientos responded with force. The Army opened fire on the strikers, killing 26 of them, after which the strike was broken.

Che's diary at the time was like a surveyor's notebook, while also like that of a lone ranger absorbed

The *guerrilleros*' diet alternated between starvation and occasional opportunities to gorge themselves. It was unusual to meet local people with food to sell them.

all the same characteristics as a guerrilla army: homogeneity, respect for their chief, bravery... But they don't have the support of the people – and so it's inevitable that they'll be caught or exterminated by the public forces.' In Bolivia, the art of insurrection was almost destined to fail because of the nature of the terrain. Theirs was very clearly a military force from another time, facing one of the bloodiest combinations of the century: a Latin American Army backed by the CIA. The war of the guerrillas against power – aspiring to become the germ of revolution on a continental scale – was so unequal that, almost by default, its members take on the romantic aura of a band of just avengers. The guerrillas went into the middle of nowhere only to be betrayed by reality, which is the same as saying, by their own lack of realism. But it was precisely that denial of reality that gave them their mythical stature: their struggle stands for all the other noble and unsuccessful battles that mankind has lost.

Today, following the defeat of many popular struggles, it may seem very easy to dismiss Che's project in Bolivia as irrational. A revolutionary act can only be legitimized by success. The first questions to ask about any insurrection are: who should bear the arms, and who will defend the people, and from whom?

Che's last political work, his 'Message to the Tricontinental', began with a quote from José Martí: '[...] this is the hour of the furnaces [...] and we need see nothing more than light.' The Bolivian experience ended in disaster but fortunately, the story does not end with the century. Far from the hour of the furnaces, when the passing of utopias seems to have extinguished any possibility of transforming the world, it is opportune to return to Che's certainty: 'I am right, we can win a war like this one (and we will).' On that day we will speak another language, and our weapons will be different.

La Higuera was Che's Night in the Garden of Gethsemane. He awaited a death in which he still could not quite believe. Thirty minutes before midnight on October 9th, Captain Prado received the telegram with the decision that had been reached. President Barrientos gave the order to execute the detainees. Prado only had to wait until the morning, when Colonel Joaquín Zenteno Anaya would arrive by helicopter. For the chance eyewitnesses of La Higuera, and all of those who were present at his death – the little schoolteacher who brought Che some soup, the soldier who cleaned his wounds, the priest who hurried in vain to hear a confession Che

The tumbledown shack belonging to Honorato Rojas, the peasant who twice betrayed the group, and led the rearguard into the ambush at Vado del Yeso.

Epifania, the 'old lady with the goats', mentioned in Che's last diary entry. In spite of their fears about her, she never betrayed the *guerrilleros*.

Three of the Cubans – Pombo, Benigno and Urbano, together with the Bolivians, Inti and Dario – were able to get through the military line: they were the only members of the group to survive.

October 3rd 1967. The arrest of Orlando Jiménez Bazán, known as "Camba". On the right, Captain Gary Prado, head of the unit that clashed with the guerrillas in Quebrada del Yuro.

would never have made – life would change. They lived to tell how they stumbled on that historic scene, and how Bolivia transformed the executed guerrilla into a Christian martyr.

It is a clear Sunday morning. A few hours before the murder three pictures are taken of the prisoner, using the Pentax belonging to the CIA agent Félix Rodríguez. The Bolivian government would only reveal the photos some decades later, since they prove that Che was not killed in battle, but executed. His hands are handcuffed together over his stomach, his hair tied back in a ponytail like a horse's mane, and his chest is bare – there are no buttons left on his shirt. Those in power have disarmed the guerrilla to turn him into a convict: the portrait is of the *guerrillero* as a social bandit. The event was not intended to be seen as a military victory, but as the arrest of a common criminal. The rebel was left unprotected under the sun. Che had written movingly romantic lines about the nocturnal character of the *guerrillero*. To be in the sun was the same as defeat, and both events sharpened the shadows on his face. Che does not look at the camera. His life is ending, and with it that photogenic quality which photos taken during the Revolution had made central to his story. But where photographs are concerned, this script has a double ending.

The sun shines through the windows of the schoolhouse. In the next room, Chang and Cuba are shot. Sergeant Mario Terán, whose entire life has passed by that morning, volunteers to carry out the sentence. But when he has to enter the room, he is quivering with fear. Che is seated on the floor with his back to the wall. His wounds have stopped bleeding. He sees his executioner shaking and urges him on: 'Fire, coward, you're going to kill a man.' The boy steps back, closes his eyes, and opens fire. There is a second burst, then another soldier joins in with a final shot. October 9th, 1967. It is 1.10 in the afternoon.

La Higuera, Bolivia.

October 9th. The last photos taken of Che alive. The decision to murder him had already been taken. The CIA agent, Félix Rodriguez, wanted to be photographed at Che's side: it was his way of finding a place in history at any price.

CHE LOOKED AT ME IN SUCH A GENTLE WAY, WITH [SUCH] A LOOK OF GRATITUDE THAT I'LL NEVER BE ABLE TO FORGET HOW HE LOOKED AT ME.

THE SOLDIERS DIDN'T LOOK AT ME LIKE THAT. [NINFA BREAKS INTO TEARS.] WHEN I HAVE A REAL PROBLEM, I CALL FOR HIM, I SEE HIS LOOK, AND HE ANSWERS ME. HE ALWAYS HELPS ME.

Ninfa Arteaga, a peasant woman from La Higuera; statement recorded by Adys Cupull and Froilán González.

187

THE PURE BEAUTY OF DEATH

On the evening of October 9th Che's body was covered in a tarpaulin and strapped to the landing gear of a helicopter, to be flown to the town of Vallegrande. In the washroom of the Nuestro Señor de Malta hospital, two men and a nurse cleaned Che's corpse and trimmed his hair to make him look more presentable. Civilian hands carried out the dignified procedure of the funeral rites that the military had disregarded. The body was injected with formaldehyde to prepare it to be seen by the local people. Gary Prado says that 'they wanted to show that this was Che, to be able to say "Here he is – we've won!"' The peasants' ingrained religiosity, and a vague feeling of collective guilt, would eventually turn what had originally been conceived as a textbook military display into a scene steeped in Christian imagery.

The population filed silently past to look upon the prophet whose strange parables they had not been able to understood. A woman cut off a lock of hair to make a secular reliquary. Later on, after her death, friends to whom she had left the lock donated it to the Museum of the Cuban Revolution. 'I didn't set out to give the image a Christian dimension,' recalled Freddy Alborta, the photographer whose shots were sent around the world by United Press International. 'I limited myself to portraying the atmosphere. There really was a solemn and mystical air about Che.'

The sparseness of the scene highlights the significance of every element. The washbasin, reminiscent of the fonts where Catholics baptize their children, and of those where the Jewish bathe their dead. Everything about the setting implies a beginning, the unveiling of a mystery suspended in immanence. This is an archetype of a death in the West, an image at zero degrees, timeless and placeless: his gaze, indifferent and absent, the disdain of his smile, the faucet that points to his genitals, and to his *guerrillero*'s feet. It says: this is a body. Or more exactly: this is a body used as a propaganda pamphlet, but to such effect that it outshines the uniforms of its murderers. The murderers represent the event. Only the police can believe

NOW I CAN'T ASK MY
COMANDANTE FOR ORDERS;
HE'S NO LONGER THERE TO REPLY;
HE'S ALREADY GIVEN HIS ANSWER.
WE MUST REMEMBER IT, OR GUESS
IT, OR INVENT WHICH STEPS TO
TAKE TOWARDS OUR OWN DESTINY.

Francisco Urondo, "Descarga"
('Shot')

Mantegna's Dead Christ.

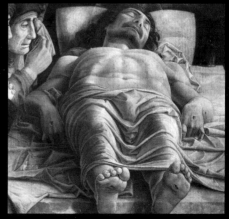

★

The Bolivian President, René Barrientos, announces the destruction of the guerrilla group to the country. At his side, General Alfredo Ovando, Chief of the Armed Forces.

Che's body strapped to the helicopter's skids, before being taken from La Higuera to Vallegrande.

that Che has died, and that makes them loathsome. And obscene. In his final, absent, pose, Che's will and his destiny have come together, as they do for all heroes. His serene cadaver convinces us of the pure beauty of death: he promises to wake again.

Che's personal effects were divided up like the spoils of war. Colonel Zenteno Anaya kept Che's Garand rifle; CIA agent Félix Rodríguez ended up with his bag of tobacco and one of the watches Che wore – an Oyster Rolex that had been given to him by the Cuban government. A second Rolex had belonged to the fallen rebel known as 'Tuma', who entrusted it to the *Comandante* to give to his Cuban family; it was kept by Lieutenant Colonel Andrés Selich. Che's executioner was left with only a pipe.

On October 10th, Zenteno Anaya hurriedly called a press conference which carried news of Che's death around the world. At first, the legend of the invincible guerrilla fighter made it difficult for left-wing activists to believe that he was dead. That is why so much importance was given to photos of the dead man – dozens of pictures were taken. Illogical as it may seem, the sheets of negatives were intended not only to confirm the rigor mortis but also to remove any sense of Che's reality.

Alborta was the midwife to Che's immortality. In a brief but illuminating essay, British critic John Berger compares the composition of the Bolivian's photographs with that of two classic paintings, Rembrandt's *Doctor Tulp's Anatomy Lesson*, and Mantegna's *Christ*: 'In certain rare cases, the tragedy of a man's death completes and exemplifies the meaning of his entire life. I am acutely aware of that in respect of Che, as certain painters were

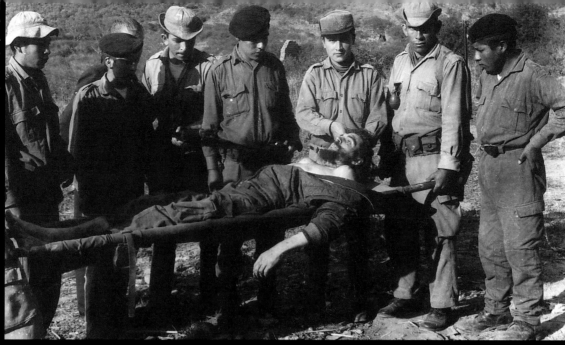

Soldiers removing Che's body from the tiny school in La Higuera, where he was executed. Mid-day on October 9th.

The first of the onlookers collect around the laundry of the "Nuestro Señor de Malta" hospital in Vallegrande.

Some 30 photographers representing the international media were taken by the Army to the hospital laundry in Vallegrande. On October 10th 1967 the UPI news agency flooded the world with the images captured by Freddy Alborta.

Roberto Guevara, Che's brother, arrived in Vallegrande on October 10th to reclaim his remains. He was not allowed to see Che.

once aware of it about Christ. That is the degree of emotional correspondence.' And yet, if the photo was attempting to reproduce his death, and to relegate Che to history, its enormous reserves of myth ensured that the art of photography would achieve the opposite effect. Alborta's traditional portrait composition – a composition rooted in the collective imaginary of the West – relates his photographs to classical representations of Jesus.

The whole of Che's diary was photographed. Some weeks later, the Bolivian government put the originals of *The Complete Bolivian Diaries of Che Guevara* on sale. Even while contracts were being prepared with the big international agencies, other deals were underway. The Bolivian Minister of the Interior, Antonio Arguedas, obtained a microfilm of the diary and passed it over to Cuba. This meant that in the end Havana had priority in publishing Che's last text. *The Bolivian Diaries*. Their endorsement of *Guevarist* theory became cult reading for young people the world over, and the epic story they told contributed to bringing about historically unprecedented advances for an entire generation. Together with Alborta's photographs, they offered irrefutable proof that political commitment and the purging of individualism should be carried to their ultimate consequences, not excluding death itself.

Roberto Guevara, a lawyer, traveled to Vallegrande on October 10th to demand his brother's remains. He was told that he could not see the body because it had been cremated. In the hours that followed the murder, the

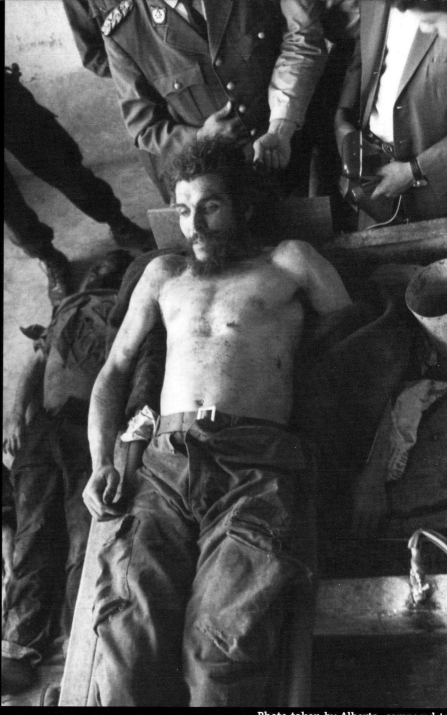

Photo taken by Alborta, compared to Mantegna's 'Dead Christ'.

A MAN FOR EVERY BEGINNING,

[AND] FOR THE ULTIMATE TEST, OF

FINDING ONESELF WITH A SINGLE

DEATH, TO MARK THAT DEATH,

STONE UPON STONE, EACH STONE

BUILDING THE FIRE...

military leaders had been having an
extensive debate over what should
happen to the body. It soon became
clear that it would not be buried in
Bolivia, nor returned to Havana.
Either of those options would have added to Che's status as a political
martyr. The preferred option was cremation. While Vallegrande's residents
were filing past the body, the officers were searching in vain for an oven
where they might reduce it to ashes. In a book that had a limited circulation,
General Arnaldo Saucedo asserts that only practical difficulties had prevented
the cremation from being carried out. They opted for a less macabre method
of 'disappearance' – namely a clandestine burial in a common grave. By this
point, several of Che's *compañeros* had been captured, and condemned to the
same fate as their leader. Meanwhile, Havana was still waiting to receive
positive proof of the dead man's identity. General Alfredo Ovando Candia
proposed decapitating him and preserving his head in formaldehyde. His
suggestion was not adopted: the Cuban CIA agent thought that one finger
would be enough. Their differences were resolved in a manner worthy of King
Solomon. Once the public display was over, both of Che's hands were cut off
and preserved in a formaldehyde jar. However, Antonio Arguedas managed to
steal them, and sent them to Cuba together with the microfilm.

In the days that followed, only a few of the rebels managed to avoid

FROM HIM WE HOPED FOR ALL

THE DARTS OF POSSIBILITY,

AND NOW WE EXPECT ALL THE

RICHNESS OF FANTASY.

José Lezama Lima Ernesto Guevara,
comandante nuestro.
('Ernesto Guevara, our leader')

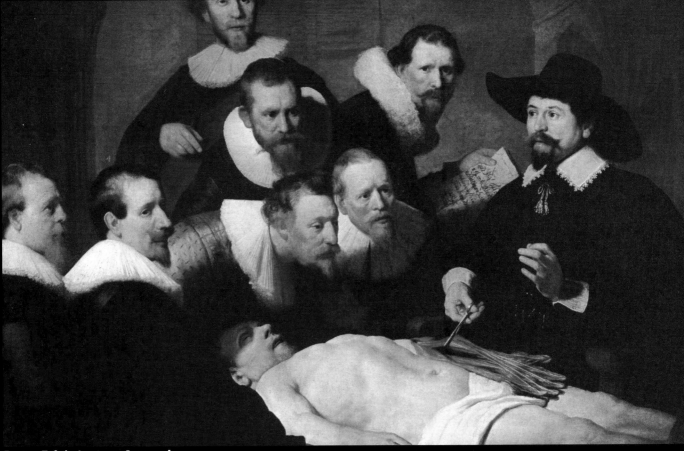

Doctor Tulp's Anatomy Lesson, by Rembrandt. The images (above and below) fulfil a similar purpose: both try to portray a corpse as if it is being formally and objectively examined...

capture by the soldiers. In all, there were three Cubans – Pombo, Benigno and Leonardo Tamayo (alias Urbano) – together with Inti Peredo and Darío Méndez. They were eventually helped on their way to Chile by the Bolivian Communist Party, where they came under the protection of the future President, Senator Salvador Allende, who had close ties to the Cuban Revolution.

For three decades the people of south-east Bolivia have placed flowers in the laundry of the Nuestro Señor de Malta hospital. They have cried for themselves, and for the leader they had adopted as a martyr. They call him St Ernesto of La Higuera. The place remains today just as it was then, except for the walls covered with graffiti honoring the Absent One. The washroom has become an unusually solemn shrine, and a home to the ghost of history. During the government of General Juan José Torres, the residents of Vallegrande renamed the street leading to the cemetery as 'Che Guevara Avenue'. With the next *coup* it was renamed 'Army Avenue', although according to Pastor Aguilar, a local journalist, 'everyone knows it's still called Che Guevara Avenue'.

The revolutionary had made clear that he would not want to have a

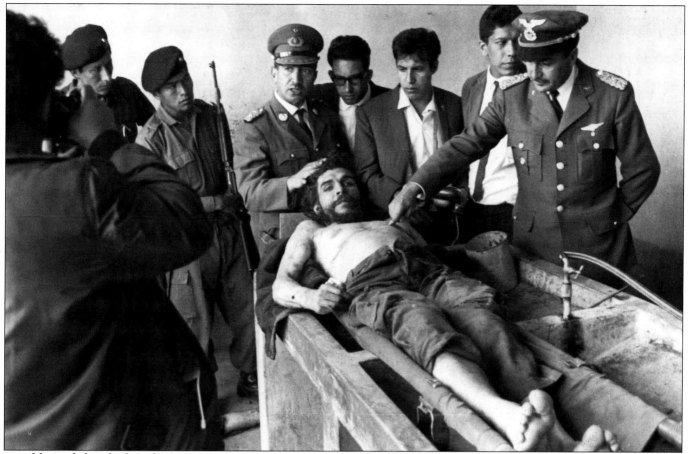

...and beyond that, both seek to use a dead person as an example: in one case, to advance medicine, in the other, as a political warning."
John Berger

special grave, for the same reason that a myth can only be created far from home, that no one is a prophet in his own land. The proverb captures the bundle of enigmas needed to make a real person into a legend. On this topic, Borrego is – finally – quite explicit, in saying that: 'Che, a Christian? My ass. Che wasn't defeated in La Higuera. He was reborn there'. There he is, a joking Che, chuckling to himself, like the Mona Lisa. And so, to prevent his final image from being tarnished by our solemnity, or by Holbein or Rembrandt, it's worth recalling that image of him laughing out loud in the anatomy lesson at the University of Buenos Aires, as he confronted another dead body. In the realm of biography, it is the exceptional person who remains true to the fantasies of their childhood. In the realm of myth, the hero always receives destiny's mandate in his youth. Comedy is the last resort of an anti-hero, and some comedies depend on black humor. Che laughed even then at his own death, just as the dead man would finally laugh at his enemies. They never imagined he would take so long to die. But he who laughs last, laughs longest.

The dead Christ, **Holbein the younger.**

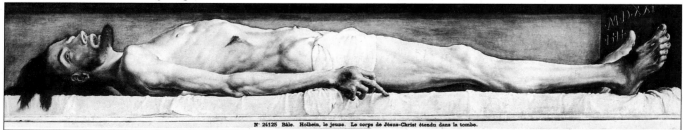

N° 24125 Bâle. Holbein, le jeune. Le corps de Jésus-Christ étendu dans la tombe.

CHE IN THE SKY WITH RIFLES

On the night of October 18th, before a million citizens of Havana assembled in the Plaza of the Revolution, Fidel Castro opened the service of commemoration to the 'Heroic *Guerrillero*'. In an act which had all the grandiloquent scenery and emotional intensity of an opera – and for Che, no less, who was an aesthete – Castro paid tribute to one of the most passionate and controversial friendships of the century, repaying the *compañero* who had achieved legendary status for his past vicissitudes in the exercise of power. He was also bidding a resounding farewell to the most romantic chapter of the Cuban Revolution, as Ernesto 'Che' Guevara ascended into the national pantheon.

'If we want to express how we want the men of future generations to be, we must say: Be like Che! If we want to say how we would like our children to be educated, we should say without hesitation: We want them to be educated in the spirit of Che!' Fidel's words made Che Cuban again, recording his guerrilla struggle in the nation's history, at the center of patriotic fervor.

Both within Cuba and elsewhere, the icon is inseparable from one image: the portrait taken by Cuban photographer Alberto Díaz 'Korda' (see p. 198). To understand this phenomenon we have to return to the early years of the Revolution, to the 1950s, when Korda was a young advertising photographer who took pictures of models for the covers of weekly magazines. The triumph of the Cuban Revolution attracted him into the streets for the first time, to register the collective euphoria. Within a year he had given up his studio to work as a photographic journalist for the newspaper *Revolución*. On March 4th 1960 when the French freighter *La Coubre* was blown up in Havana harbor, Fidel immediately accused the CIA of sabotage. One day later the government carried out an act of public mourning and Korda covered the event. After taking photos of the speakers, he scanned the platform with his Leika. And quite unexpectedly, Che entered his visual field for 15 seconds, leaning on the railing. The photographer snapped twice. Korda recalls that

Dozens of photos of their father pass through Che's children's hands in the October 1967 issue of Bohemia.

parades, and solemn slides projected onto huge screens. Just a few months earlier, Castro had publicly supported the Soviet invasion of Czechoslovakia. But these were years that did not encourage dispute, preferring instead the unifying theme of official discourse. It is not surprising that Cuba would shortly enter what became known as 'the gray half-decade'.

Che Guevara became one of the patriotic sources of the new school. Even today, children between fourth and seventh grade are 'pioneers'. The anthem they sing every morning in the school yard is 'Pioneers for Communism/ We will be like Che.' In the national firmament, while Camilo Cienfuegos stands out for his human and prosaic qualities, Che is presented as a man 'without flaws'.

In the 1970s, artists such as sculptors and ceramicists, worked over Che's portraits to experiment with variations on a heroic theme. His image was be the leitmotif of the Cuban poster, a movement that drew on virtually every possible aesthetic – from op-art to afro, indigenist imagery to psychodelia – with the notable exception of Soviet socialist realism. Artist Raúl Martínez employed the most popular images of Che in the pop art designs he brought to Cuba.

The *guerrillero*'s beauty was gradually drained of its eroticism. His narcissistic seductiveness, a presence to be seen in any of his photos, was pushed into the background in order to perfect the ideal and create a universal archetype. His youthful face gained shadows under the eyes, in keeping with his nocturnal and watchful qualities. 'Cubanization' restored the contradictions in his make-up as the standard-bearer of proletarian internationalism. In the Plaza de la Revolución, his wrought-iron profile hangs from the façade of the functionalist Ministry of the Interior. Didactic in purpose, the portrait tries to restrain Che without quite disowning him: it is a fossilized image.

Nonetheless, even the state-sponsored cult could not contain the people's adoration for Che. How could the people not appropriate Camilo and Che in life-size wax models, standing beside their embalmed mules in the Museum of the Revolution? The former is charming, as always; Che is smiling and athletic. They seem less like two *guerrilleros* than a couple of adorable villains from a Latin American cowboy film. In this secular yet Christian country, it is interesting to see how much religious sentiment has effectively come to be represented by the figure of Che. His portrait decorates many public offices, and many Cubans are married beneath his photo, which hangs in the place that Catholic countries reserve for a cross.

Korda's portrait has become like a mantra painted on the walls and fences of Havana. Che's figure is lit up and put out again according to the

Che next to a protrait of José Martí, martyr of Cuban Independence.

Che in the work of Raúl Martínez.

A three peso coin.

needs of the moment. Like every idol, his silence speaks to us and his look makes a judgement. He symbolizes the beginnings of the State and, at the same time, provides an unassailable model of conduct: 'The best homage is to be seen in the everyday struggle.' Even today, TV adverts show Che setting an example with his wheelbarrow, doing voluntary work. Although a handful of intellectuals are beginning to dethrone him, most Cubans continue to love Che. They have been trained in that love, and in worshipping Che, they also become aware of the weaknesses of other leaders.

Che's portrait on the souvenir stands represents an outstanding example of State kitsch: his icon can be found on a corkscrew, a pair of maracas or a shell, with 'Souvenir of Cuba' written beneath. In recent years, Cubans have lived through – 'suffered' might be more appropriate – the dismantling of the old Communist system. The fall of the Berlin Wall and the brutal US trade embargo have reduced the Cuban leadership's room for maneuver. The market economy has opened up a broad space that often gives rise to bizarre forms of trade, and certain citizens of Havana have been known to ply their wares on unsuspecting tourists. The classic souvenir, for instance, is the Cuban three peso coin bearing Che's image. It now has a face value of only about 15 cents, but tourists will buy them for a dollar each.

In the 1960s the island was the cradle of an internationalist utopia, and as such a political laboratory for the rest of the world: what Cuba began had a major influence. After Che's death, his image became the emblem of that utopia, and his face the purest and most productive means of spreading that ideology. Emerging from the cultural hegemony of the Cuban Revolution, the Che's revolutionary aura overflowed its origins to spread across the entire world. Liberation struggles worldwide amplified his myth, disseminating it widely.

A memorial gathering on the first anniversary of his death. In Cuba, 1968 was declared "The year of the heroic guerrillero".

And now a word about Che as an ideologue. We have already mentioned the letter he sent to the Tricontinental meeting: 'Our motto is: Create two, three... many Vietnams!' After his death, this text became his revolutionary testament, an anti-imperialist manifesto addressed to the entire Third World. Che's political writings formed a theory that was oriented towards immediate action. They were an agitator's essays, and like the tales of his guerrilla experience, they were all written in simple language and deployed the emotional rhetoric of political pamphlets. Che disagreed strongly with the pro-Soviet Communist parties – which argued the need to 'wait until the conditions for revolution are ripe'. He took the view that it should be possible either to create or at least speed up historical processes. His crucial contribution was the notion of a guerrilla vanguard: a small, armed, advance force that could blitz its way through to secure popular liberation.

Images of Che in Havana.

The First Congress of the Cuban Communist Party, 1975. Marx, Engels and Lenin together with the Fathers of Cuban Independence and the founders of the new state.

In outer space... On a Soviet space mission the Cuban cosmonaut Arnaldo Tamayo Mendéz left a marble statue of Che in orbit.

This conclusion, taken directly from the Cuban experience, was often simplified so as to apply to any historical situation. While the experience of popular struggle has revealed the voluntarist blemishes in this idea, the collapse of the *Guevarist* utopia is also closely linked to the failure of the vanguard as the motor of transformation.

In 1960 Jean-Paul Sartre proclaimed Marxism to be 'the unbeatable philosophy of our time'. At the beginning of the decade, an explosive growth in university enrolment – especially in humanities degrees – had already begun. This trend gave a radical bent to political dynamics in which young people would play an unprecedented role. Che Guevara was already the revolutionary model for Latin American activists. Revolution was the cry of the hour; and 1968 was the year in which students rebelled and were repressed. In May, Che could be seen in the banners of the Parisian *manifestations*, and again in the Italian protests, when students come together with workers to bring about massive strikes. The European student explosion had a vast cultural impact on the following decades, though in the end it was an almost victimless revolution.

The true theater of Che's influence was Latin

Che fulfils many different functions in Havana. Here he is seen in the company of St George, and the tango singer, Carlos Gardel.

America. On October 2nd 1968, during a massive student protest in the Plaza Tlatelolco in Mexico City, nearly 300 students were massacred. The region as a whole would eventually pay for its passion with the deaths of tens of thousands of activists, although their murders should be attributed to State terrorism rather than a few influential texts or romantic images. With Cuban support, a wing of Marxism that had already become known as *Guevarism* drove forward the guerrilla struggle in Latin America. Different national variations included the Chilean MIR, the Colombian M-19, as well as several armed groups in Central America. Many were founded following personal contacts with Che in the early 1960s. He had a crucial influence on the the founding of several guerrilla organizations, most of which, like the Uruguayan *Tupamaros* led by Raúl Sendic, operated in the cities.

As years pass, a gap can appear between what we originally *read* and what we originally *understood*; the paradigm adapts in order to survive. This

Consulting room of a traumatologist in Havana: with an image of Che to give inspiration.

explains why the Latin American Left came to adopt an increasingly free interpretation of Che's writings, moving away from a defense of armed struggle towards the spirit of an egalitarian utopia, particularly within the ranks of the younger militants.

As the political wheel turned, when the *Sandinista* Revolution in Nicaragua triumphed in 1979 it adopted the figure of Che, who was a 'Sandinista' of the 1950s. Working from a significant urban base, the new guerrillas took their inspiration

The many meanings
of a glance: the
Cuban Revolution as a
political paradigm of
the 1960s and Che
the model activist.

from him but had not followed his methods. In Peru, a
country with a long tradition of popular struggles, the
1980s saw the emergence of *Sendero Luminoso*, a
guerrilla group which emerged from the University of
Ayacucho and was defined as 'Maoist, Marxist, and
Guevarist' – in no particular order. In the meantime, in
another part of the same country, the *Túpac Amaru*
Revolutionary Movement was reclaiming Che in a more
traditional way. He had represented the essential and
most successful moment of the popular insurrection,
before it was contaminated by political deals about
integration, or indeed by the added component of urban
terrorism. Che embodied the classical style of guerrilla
warfare, which by the 1980s had become outmoded.

Che was not executed in Bolivia: he died as he was
returning to his own country. It was in Prague, before
leaving for his final destination, that Che told his
bodyguard, Ulises Estrada, 'I want to die with at least
one foot in my own country.' One of his unaccomplished
goals, which he had been working on since 1959, was to
set up a guerrilla *foco* in Argentina. His unsuccessful
attempt to return was subsequently taken up by the
political vanguard of the 1970s in a series of attempts
that were eventually smothered by bloody repression.
One entirely Argentinian guerrilla group of *Guevarist*
inspiration operated in the country for several years. Led

Mexico, the Plaza de las Tres Culturas.
Shortly afterwards, the scene of the
massacre of students on October 2nd 1968.

by Roberto Mario Santucho, the *Ejército Revolucionario del Pueblo* (The People's Revolutionary Army or ERP) combined rural armed struggle in the north-western province of Tucumán with attacks on urban army barracks. In March 1976 the coup led by Jorge Rafael Videla plunged the country into a bloodbath. Having been defeated militarily, the ERP broke apart in 1977 following the death of its leader Within the context of intense political radicalization, thousands of Argentinians joined guerrilla groups, although only a tiny fraction of them actually participated in armed activities. The repression, however, extended to reach all the groups, activists and union delegates who were operating openly, and ultimately took in anyone who even theoretically sympathized with revolution. In some sense, the repressive tradition of making the opposition 'disappear' began in Argentina with the guerrilla fighter Jorge Masetti, whose body was never found. Having been adopted by Bolivian officers, the technique was also employed with Ernesto Guevara de la Serna. They are among the first links in the chain of the 30,000 men and women who disappeared.

In the final analysis, Che, like Masetti, had gone off

John Lennon of the Beatles protests against the war in Vietnam from the cover of *Ramparts*, a US leftwing magazine. 10th October 1967.

May 1968, Paris. Students "taking heaven by storm...";

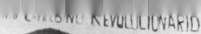

Che's image in support of the Mapuche women's demands for "Land or death". Chile 1971.

to war and their deaths were 'within the range of probability'. A form of witch-hunt continued with his family in Buenos Aires. In 1964, shortly after entering a sanitarium when she was terminally ill, Che's mother Celia de la Serna was obliged to leave when they realized who she was. Persecuted, imprisoned or exiled, every one of Che's four siblings could give testimony of what it meant to bear his name. They embody the tragedy that befell so many Argentinian families, the horror of the two letters that paradoxically identify the absence of identity: N.N. – the security forces' abbreviation for 'unidentified' persons.

The *maté* Che used as a sign of his foreignness, his habit of reading the *gaucho* poets, his characteristic irony, a certain physical arrogance, a highly developed sense of the ridiculous: all of these make up the Argentinian attributes of Che Guevara. His entire myth fits into that body, which has been tirelessly disciplined against all forms of weakness, martyred by repression, and reviled: how many more times will it be buried and exhumed yet again?

Now times are different. The political utopia of the 1970s did not exhaust the legend; it was transformed into a password. The changing generations first drove Che to the heaven of revolutionary heroes, and now bring him into the consumer marketplace, into everyday life. In the 1980s, the market recycled its most stern critic, making use of its machinery for king-making. But when Che appears as a logo, he always seems to

The ERP (Revolutionary People's Army), a *Guevarist* guerrilla organisation of the 1970s. José de San Martín, "The Liberator", provides the context for an underground press conference, 1971.

Nicaragua, 1979.

BEFORE THE IMAGES OF AUGUSTO SANDINO AND ERNESTO CHE GUEVARA, AND THE MEMORY OF THE HEROES AND MARTYRS OF NICARAGUA, LATIN AMERICA, AND ALL HUMANITY, BEFORE HISTORY, I PLACE MY HAND ON THE RED AND BLACK FLAG, TO SYMBOLIZE 'FREEDOM FOR OUR LAND, OR DEATH'.

Oath taken by the Frente Sandinista

outshine the product. Although his public significance is remembered in Cuba, in the capitalist world he endures mainly as a central motif in youth counterculture. His poster marks the liberated territory of a teenager's bedroom. While Che did not start teenage imagery by himself, several of its key elements can be found in his legacy: the urge to travel, his anti-establishment feelings, the ideal of a splendidly romantic death, all held together by a certain 'nocturnal' look. A rebel 'style' that has nothing trivial about it, given that icons only *appear* to be transient. That small world of images is reflected in the installations created by the Argentinian artist Liliana Porter, in which Che becomes a cute Mickey Mouse figure for teenagers. The advertising slogan of the English 'Che' beer lets slip a self-parodying ironic quip that renders the guerrilla an homage in keeping with postmodern taste: 'Sales banned in the US. Must be good....'

The military coup against the Socialist president, Salvador Allende. Chile, 11 September 1973.

Was everything already there to be seen in Korda's photo? (see p. 198) The jacket is in black leather, with a shiny zipper; putting Che several years ahead of the 'Easy Riders' of film fame, crossing the American West on motorbikes. Although as a result of his upbringing and his outlook Che subscribed to a chapter in sexual mores

Sipping *maté* on an unmade bed, 1960. Che provoked erotic fantasies, as well as political consciousness.

that is now closing in the West, his image foretold a change in the male image. His beret with the star and his uncombed hair prefigure the coming of androgynous chic. Although he epitomises maleness, he nonetheless heralds a profound change in masculinity. Is it not this strange destiny that we are shown again by Korda, in the beautiful cinematic sequence from the 1960 fishing championship? (see p. 102). This shows the man's most feminine side, his slightly freckled back, tremendously vulnerable, which his hair brushes in a caress.

LYING THERE YOU SMILE SERENELY, AS IF A WOMAN

WAS KISSING HIDDEN PARTS OF YOUR BODY (...)

YOUR NECK IS SEXIER THAN THE SAD NECKS OF

JOHNSON OR DE GAULLE OR KOSYGIN OR THE

BULLET-SHATTERED NECK OF JOHN KENNEDY.

Allen Ginsberg. "Elegy for Che Guevara."

1965 Flashback

Che is in a miserable appartment in Prague, with a
Beatles song playing on the portable record player. He
has finally taken to the music of the young British pop
singers. Didn't they subsequently hand out photos of Che
at one of their concerts? John Lennon could say 'Yes' to
Che and, at the same time, 'No' to the war in Vietnam.
From today's increasingly ambivalent standpoint, so
deeply rich in disappointments, kids are bringing the
guerrillero back as an anti-hero within the youngest
industry of all – pop music. Che's presence at rock
concerts and on the banners of soccer teams in Germany,
Italy and Argentina is not coincidental. Rock concerts
are the liturgical center of youth culture, the dream
factories forever in thrall to the market, where the most
developed form of consumption – the music industry –
leaves its mark. In societies addicted to football, your
team gives you a powerful sense of belonging, a second
home chosen in childhood within the cosy setting of the

A change of genre. La
Giaconda, in Reineiro
Tamayo's montage.

Andrés Calamaro, a popular
Argentine rock musician.

COME ON, YOU FLEAS!*

TAKE AN EGG TO THE FRONT

'COS EVERYONE WILL ASK YOU.

A FLAG

THAT SAYS CHE GUEVARA

A COUPLE OF ROCK 'N' ROLL SONGS

AND A JOINT TO SMOKE.

KILLING A PIG**

WILL PAY FOR WALTER.***

ALL OVER ARGENTINA

THE CARNIVAL BEGINS.

Name of a rock group
** 'Rati' is slang for 'cop'*
*** Walter Bulacio, killed by the police*
following a rock concert.*

family. Nothing is trivial in this environment and Che is entirely at home in the huge stadiums, those modern theaters of confrontation between kids and authority, between power and the people. Che is where the kids are. His image guarantees a marvelous degree of... chaos.

At the same time, it is again in Latin America – in the same Mexico that witnessed his political baptism – that Che is returning in a way that is faithful both to the hero and anti-hero. If Che was a *Zapatista* in the 1950s, it is *Subcomandante* Marcos, the leader of the indigenous uprising in the Lacandona forest in Chiapas, Mexico, who now returns to his utopia in circumstances that are bound to be less than perfect. There can be no return without change, and he is not going back to what he experienced before.

In contrast to Che's utopia, the new *Zapatismo* was not proposing to seize power but to ensure the full operation of democracy in a country that was currently under one-party rule. The ability to attract Che to return therefore is a sign of realism and of the lessons learnt from earlier struggles. The *Ejército Zapatista de Liberación Nacional* (the Zapatista Army of National Liberation - EZLN) was having to resolve a number of serious conceptual dilemmas. In the media-driven society, those responsible for conducting armed struggles cannot neglect the popular consensus, which is heavily influenced by the images presented on radio, TV and in the press. When you wear a ski mask to cover your face (see p. 214), as a kind of magic for the TV cameras, then Che has to be 'packaged' to give a more 'politically correct' image. But *Subcomandante* Marcos has not lost his romanticism by becoming a realist. On the contrary: he recognizes that realism is an inherent part of every popular uprising. The EZLN looked for a language that would let the guerrillas retain what is still worth keeping from their anachronism: a language that marks a watershed between their future and their classical tradition.

"*Chaca* or death! We will overcome!"
Flag of the Argentine football club, the Chacarita Juniors.

Che's effigy, a symbol of solidarity and a challenge to the
police in football stadia.

From a remote village called La Realidad ('Reality'), the *Subcomandante* takes the microphone to vindicate Che's poetics: 'I've been looking for a quote to back up my opening words at this meeting. I've gone from Pablo Neruda to Julio Cortázar, from Walt Whitman to Juan Rulfo. It was a waste of time. Again and again the image of Che dreaming in the schoolhouse in La Higuera demanded it should take its place between my hands. From Bolivia came those half-closed eyes and that ironic smile to tell us what was happening now, and to promise what would happen in the future. Did I say 'dreaming'? Should I have said 'dead?' For some he died, but for others, he only fell asleep.'

Poetics, then. There is little to be gained from regretting the distortions to the model of Che. History will decide how he endures. The twentieth century has ended before the voyager reaches the destination. But Che's name has become an irrevocable part of the utopian tradition, and his spirit continues to call us to join the adventure of transforming the world.

Sub-comandante Marcos and new resources for the popular insurrection: ski mask, cell phone, and Che for his poetry.

CHE REMINDS US OF WHAT WE'VE

KNOWN FROM THE TIME OF

SPARTACUS, BUT SOMETIMES

FORGET: THAT IN THE FIGHT

AGAINST INJUSTICE, HUMANITY

DISCOVERS A STEP THAT TAKES IT

HIGHER, MAKES IT BETTER,

CHANGES IT INTO SOMETHING THAT

IS MORE HUMAN.

Subcomandante Marcos,
April 4th 1994

POSTSCRIPT

The washhouse in Vallegrande, where Che's body was displayed. A place of worship for the Cult of San Ernesto de La Higuera.

Towards the end of 1995, General Mario Vargas Salinas, who led the operation that ended the guerrilla campaign at Vado del Yeso, refuted the official claim that Che had been cremated. A team of Cuban and Argentinian forensic anthropologists immediately began the search for a communal grave, whose location alongside the landing strip at the local airport had long been an open secret in Vallegrande. Their work progressed in short bursts which were complicated by false leads, army infighting and diplomatic wrangles. However in June 1997, almost three decades after Che's murder, the search began to show results.

Ernesto Guevara de la Serna: communal grave No 9. A body with bare feet, crippled legs, and no hands. The respiratory fatigue Che suffered since infancy had left clear signs on his skull, and the technique of photographic superimposition removed any remaining doubts about his identity. With revolutionary zeal – and a fear that his precious find might be taken from him – Jorge González, the senior member of the Cuban forensic team, slept for one week at the burial site. And eventually he was able to touch the front of the skull and find the gap left by one of Che's molars, and could announce 'We've found the

Exhuming the common grave in Vallegrande. Che's remains were officially identified on July 12th 1997.

Late on the same day, Che was received in Cuba with full military honours.

Fidel Castro has always been ready to celebrate good news. Mythologized by the three decades in hiding, Che's remains returned to Cuba with propitious timing, just before the thirtieth anniversary of his death. While the myth that surrounded him had made Che's bones into [secular] relics, everything else connected with him suddenly seemed to be distorted by political interests. During the search, Loyola Guzmán, the young *guerrillera* who had fought alongside Che in Bolivia, had found the remains of his feet, which were to be deposited in a monument to Che in Vallegrande. Havana ensured that Che would continue to symbolize the heroism of the Cuban Revolution.

The brief ceremony to mark Che's return to Cuba, on July 12th 1997 was conducted in a family atmosphere. The body was received with military honors by the victors of the 1959 revolution. The government announced that people would be able to give tribute to Che in October, when his remains were taken to the monument dedicated to him by the city of Santa Clara, the first Cuban city Che knew. The giant statue portrays him striding forward: the *guerrillero* leading the way, his rifle ready for action, with his left arm in a sling – which may make this the only statue to portray a country's founding father in a plaster cast. While this work of socialist realism with a Cuban twist draws attention to the hero's physical weakness, it also shows his determination to overcome it.

A light breeze from the 1960s has returned to mark the end of the century in Cuba. The farewell was calm, but an apotheosis may still take place. The country was reminded of its own youth as it recovered its everlasting and powerful *guerrillero*: Ernesto 'Che' Guevara, the embodiment of incorruptibility.

FROM TIME TO TIME, SPARE A

THOUGHT FOR THIS SMALL-TIME

20TH CENTURY SOLDIER OF FORTUNE.

Che's farewell to his parents.

The monument to Che in Santa Clara, the site of his mausoleum.

HASTA LA VICTORIA SIEMPRE

CHÉ*

Liliana Porter "Che/Che" (detail), 1997, cibachrome print and assemblage.

CHRONOLOGY

1928
June 14th. Ernesto Guevara de la Cerna, the first child of Ernesto Guevara Lynch and Celia de la Cerna, is born in Rosario, Argentina.

1929
The family moves to the Province of Misiones, where they have a *maté* (herbal tea) plantation. Che's sister Celia is born.

1930
May. Ernesto has his first asthma attack, and is diagnosed as having a severe asthmatic condition.

1932
The family move to Buenos Aires. Ernesto's brother, Roberto is born.

1933
June. The family move to Alta Gracia, a small town in the Córdoba hills which has a more suitable climate for those suffering from respiratory problems. They live there until 1943.

1934
January 28th. Ernesto's second sister, Ana María, is born.

1936
Outbreak of the Spanish Civil War. Ernesto's uncle Córdova Iturburu is the war correspondent for the newspaper *Crítica*. He provides Ernesto's first direct connection with politics.

1943
Ernesto finishes his secondary school education in Córdoba, and begins a friendship with the Granado brothers and the Ferrer brothers. His youngest brother, Juan Martín, is born.

1945
The family moves to Buenos Aires, where Ernesto enrols in the Medical Faculty, and works to pay for his studies. He meets Tita Infante.

1950
January 1st. Ernesto travels more than 4,500 kms across the north of Argentina on a motorized bicycle. He spends some time in the Chañar leper colony and works for the national highway authorities and the Argentine merchant navy.
October. He meets Chichina Ferreyra, a young woman from one of Córdoba's leading families.

1951
December 29th. After saying farewell to Chichina, Ernesto sets off on a motorbike with Alberto Granado to begin his first journey to other Latin America countries. He travels through Chile, Bolivia

and Peru – where he visits the San Pablo leper colony. They travel down the Amazon River towards Colombia and Venezuela on the *Mambo-Tango* raft.

1952
August 31st. Ernesto returns to Argentina to complete his university studies.

1953
June 12th. He graduates as a doctor.
July 7th. Ernesto leaves by train for Bolivia. His farewell to his parents was: 'Another soldier of America is on his way!'
July 12th. He arrives in Bolivia at a moment of high political tension.
July 26th. Fidel Castro and other revolutionaries attack the Moncada Barracks in a unsuccessful attempt to overthrow the dictatorship of Fulgencio Batista. Ernesto spends the next few months traveling through Peru, Ecuador and Costa Rica.
December 20th. He reaches Guatemala, where he stays for nine months.
December 23rd. He meets Hilda Gadea, a Peruvian exile.
December 26th. Gadea introduces him to Cuban exiles from the July 26th Movement, among them Ñico López, who subsequently gives him the nickname 'Che'. He works *ad honorem* in a hospital.

1954
June. A military coup financed by the United States brings down the government of Jacobo Arbenz in Guatemala. Ernesto travels to Mexico.

1955
July. In Mexico he is introduced to Fidel Castro Ruz. Soon after their first meeting, he volunteers to join the Cuban expedition.
August 18th. Ernesto marries Hilda Gadea, who is expecting their child. He makes a living working as a street photographer and, briefly, by reporting on the Panamerican Games for *Agencia Latina*.

1956
February 15th. Their first child, Hilda Beatriz, is born.
April. Ernesto – 'Che' – begins military training with the Cubans. The instructor, a Spanish republican, Alberto Bayo, describes him as his most outstanding trainee.
June 24th. Che is arrested by the Mexican authorities with Fidel and other Cuban exiles, and held in the Miguel Schultz prison.
July 6th. Che tells his parents that he will be taking part in the expedition to Cuba.
July 31st. Following his release from jail he continues with his training.
November 25th. He leaves for Cuba, with 82 other men, in the overcrowded *Granma*, as a member of the *guerrilla* group's General Staff.
December 2nd. The force disembark in a mangrove

swamp. The local community leaders provide them with logistical help.
December 25th. Twenty-one members of the invasion force are killed in the Battle of Alegría del Pío.

1957
January 17th. The rebel army's first military success, as they take over the La Plata barracks. They follow this with another victory at Arroyo del Infierno.
May 28th. El Uvero – another successful attack.
July 21st. Castro promotes Che to the rank of Major, and puts him in charge of establishing the Rebel Army's' Fourth Column.
August 30th. Che leads his troops to victory in El Hombrito.
November. Publication of the first issue of the rebels' newspaper, *El Cubano Libre*.

1958
February 24th. Radio Rebelde's first broadcast. The insurgent forces begin to establish themselves, establishing their first factories and bases.
August. The columns led by Che and Camilo Cienfuegos launch the 'invasion' from the west of the island. They advance 554km in 47 days.
October. Che unites the various anti-Batista groups under his control in El Escambray, while simultaneously pushing ahead with fresh plans for agrarian reform.
December. Che meets Aleida March. While Fidel advances on Santiago de Cuba, Che launches what will prove to be the decisive attack on Santa Clara.
December 31st. Che captures Santa Clara, precipitating the end of the dictatorship.

1959
January 1st. Batista goes into exile.
January 3rd. Camilo Cienfuegos enters Havana, which has been paralysed by a general strike.
January 4th. Che reaches the capital.
January 8th. Fidel makes a victorious entry into Havana.
January 9th. Che's parents arrive in Cuba.
January 21st. Hilda Gadea and his daughter, Hildita Guevara arrive. They agree to dissolve their marriage.
February 7th. Che is awarded Cuban citizenship.
March. He is involved in drafting the Agricultural Reform Bill.
June 2nd. He marries Aleida March.
June 12th. He makes his first trip to the United Arab Republic and other Middle Eastern countries.
July 7th. He is received by Jawarlahal Nehru in New Delhi.
July 17th. He holds discussions with Tito in Yugoslavia.
October 8th. He is appointed Head of the Industries Department of the National Institute for Agrarian Reform. The decision is taken to confiscate the *latifundios* (large privately-owned estates).

October 28th. Camilo Cienfuegos is killed in a plane crash.
November 26th. Che is appointed President of the National Bank.

1960

March 5th. The photographer, Alberto Korda, takes the famous picture of Che during the homage to the victims of the steamer, *La Coubre*.
April. Che is appointed to direct the Training Department of the Revolutionary Armed Forces, and publishes *La Guerra de guerrillas* ('Guerrilla Warfare'), which he dedicates to Camilo Cienfuegos.
August 8th. He takes part in the closing ceremony of the First Latin American Youth Congress.
October 19th. The US imposes a commercial embargo on Cuba.
October 22nd. Che leads an economic delegation to the Soviet Union, Czechoslovakia, China, Korea, and the German Democratic Republic. In Berlin he meets Tamara Bunke.
November 24th. He is in China when Aleidita, his first daughter with March, is born.

1961

January 3rd. The US breaks off diplomatic relations with Cuba.
February 23rd. On being appointed Minister for Industry, Che brings hundreds of state-owned companies under central control.
April 17th. The Bay of Pigs invasion fails.
August 4th. Che leads a delegation to the Inter-American Conference in Punta del Este, Uruguay. In Montevideo he is received with offers of assistance. He makes a hell-raising speech predicting the failure of the new 'Alliance for Progress' organisation, which is open to every country in Latin America – except Cuba. After meetings with the presidents of Uruguay and Brazil, and he meets the Argentine President, Arturo Frondizi, in Buenos Aires.

1962

January. Cuba is expelled from the Organization of American States (OAS).
May 20th. Che's first son, Camilo, is born.
June. Castro agrees to Russia installing nuclear missiles in Cuba.
August 26th. Che embarks on another tour in search of economic agreements.
August 31st. Che signs the missiles agreement with Kruschev in the Crimea.
October. 'The [Cuban] Missile Crisis.' After much fierce debate on both sides, Kruschev and Kennedy agree behind the Cubans' backs to dismantle the missile bases, further increasing the gap between Che and the Soviet bloc.

1963

April. Celia de la Serna is arrested on charges of producing pro-Cuban propaganda.

June 14th. Che's fourth child is born (his third with Aleida March), and named Celia, after her grandmother.
July. Che visits Algeria.

1964

January. Castro signs a commercial agreement with Kruschev and a communiqué in favor of peaceful co-existence.
March. Che travels on a diplomatic mission to Switzerland, France, Czechoslovakia and Algeria.
April 18th. In Argentina the small 'Jorge Ricardo Masetti' guerrilla group is put out of action by the Police.
November 4th. Che leaves on a diplomatic mission to Moscow.
December 11th. Che leads the Cuban delegation to the General Assembly of the United Nations, where he delivers a fiercely anti-colonialist speech.
December 18th. He arrives in Algeria, *en route* for Tanzania, Congo-Brazzaville (now DR Congo), Egypt, Mali, Guinea, Ghana and Dahomey (now Benin).

1965

February 2nd. Che travels to China, France, Algeria, Tanzania and Egypt. The industrial development program he had been campaigning for is effectively destroyed by a trade treaty which is signed in his absence.
February 24th. While Che is flying between Cairo and Algeria, his second son, Ernesto, is born.
February 25th. His speech in Algeria is strongly critical of the Soviet bloc for failing to support the struggle to free the repressed people of the world. He stops over in Egypt on his way to the Congo (now DR Congo).
March 15th. In Cuba he is asked to account for the speech he made in Algeria. By this stage he has decided to leave Cuba for the Congo.
April 1st. He leaves Cuba under the assumed identity of Ramón Benítez.
April 14th. Celia de la Serna sends him her last letter, which he will never have the opportunity to read.
April 24th. With three Cubans he arrives in the Congo. Their small force will eventually recruit 100 volunteers.
May 19th. Celia de la Serna dies.
June. After two months of waiting, the Congolese *guerrillas* go into action for the first time.
October. In the founding ceremony of the Cuban Communist Party, Fidel reads out Che's letter of resignation from all of his official responsibilities in the Revolutionary government. Che notes in his diary that this decision will have made him a foreigner to Cubans.
November 22nd. The Cuban mission withdraws from the Congo.

1966

January. The 'Tricontinental' Congress is held in

Havana. Aleida visits Che in Tanzania, where he is living underground.
March. Che arrives in Prague under an assumed name.
July. He returns in secret to Cuba to plan the Bolivian campaign.
November 3rd. He enters Bolivia using the credential of an OAS observer.
November 7th. On reaching Ñancahuazú, Che begins his Bolivian diary.
December 31st. Mario Monje, General Secretary of the PCB (Bolivian Communist Party), visits the camp. The Party refuses to support the *guerrillas*.

1967

February 1st. The *guerrilleros* leave Ñancahuazú to reconnoitre the local area.
March 15th. Two of the combatants desert. The Army becomes aware of the group's activities.
March 19th. Che returns to the camp to find Tania, Régis Debray and Ciro Bustos.
April. The *guerrillas* record their only significant victories against the army. A message from Che is read out to the Tricontinental Congress.
April 3rd. Che divides his forces, with Joaquín leading the second column.
April 20th. Debray, Bustos and George Andrew Roth are detained by the Army.
August 14th. Soldiers raid the camp in Ñancahuazú.
August 31st. Joaquín's column is ambushed in Vado del Yeso.
October 8th. Che is wounded and captured by a group of rangers.
October 9th. Che is killed on the instructions of the Bolivian government, and with the knowledge of the CIA. The location of his remains remained a mystery for three decades. His murderers were never brought to trial.
October 18th. In Havana, a million Cubans attend the Solemn Wake in Homage to Che's memory.

1997

July 12th. Che's remains are identified in Vallegrande, and flown back to Cuba on the same day.

Bibliography

Acevedo González, Enrique, *Descamisado*, Editora Política, Havana, 1993.

Alarcón Ramírez, Dariel, *Benigno. Vie et mort de la Révolution Cubaine*, Fayard, París, 1995.

Anderson, Jon Lee, *Che Guevara: A Revolutionary Life*, Grove Press, New York, 1997.

Berger, John, "The Legendary Che Guevara Is Dead", in *New Society*, New York, 1967.

Cabrera Infante, Guillermo, "Entrela Historia y la Nada", en *Mea Cuba*, Vuelta, México, 1993.

Castañeda, Jorge, *La vida en rojo*, Planeta, Buenos Aires, 1997.

Cormier, Jean, *Mística y coraje, La vida del Che*, Editorial Sudamericana, Buenos Aires, 1997.

Cupull, Adys y González, Froilán, *Cálida presencia*, Oriente, Santiago de Cuba, 1995.

- *De Ñacahuazú a La Higuera*, © Editora Política, Havana, 1994.

- *Ernestito vivo y presente*, Editora Política, Havana, 1989.

- *Entre nosotros*, Ediciones Abril, Havana, 1992.

- *Un hombre bravo*, Editorial Capitán San Luis, Havana, 1994.

Debray, Régis, *La guérilla du Che*, Seuil, París, 1974.

- *Loués soient nos seigneurs*, Gallimard, París, 1996.

Desnoes, Edmundo, "El Che y los ojos del mundo", in *Cuba Internacional*, April, 1971.

Gadea, Hilda, *Che Guevara: Años decisivos*, Aguilar, México DF, 1972.

Guevara Lynch, Ernesto, *Mi hijo el Che*, Planeta, Barcelona, 1981.

- *Aquí va un soldado de América*, Sudamericana/Planeta, Buenos Aires, 1987.

Gambini, Hugo, *El Che Guevara, La biografía*, Planeta, 1996.

Hobsbawm, Eric, *History of the Twentieth Century*, Grijalbo, Buenos Aires, 1997.

Kalfon, Pierre, *Che: Ernesto Guevara, une légende du siècle*, Seuil, París, 1997.

Korol, Claudia, *El Che y losargentinos*, Ediciones Dialéctica, Buenos Aires, 1988.

Kunzle, David, "Uses of the Portrait: the Che Poster", in *Art in America*, September/October, 1975.

Masetti, Jorge R., *Los que luchan y los que lloran*, edición cubana, Havana, 1960.

Miná, Gianni, *Habla Fidel*, Sudamericana, Buenos Aires, 1988.

Rodríguez Herrera, Mariano, *Con la adarga albrazo*, Editora Política, Havana, 1983.

Rojas, Martha y Rodríguez Calderón, Mirta, *Tania. La guerrillera inolvidable*, Instituto del Libro, Havana, 1970.

Rojo, Ricardo, *Mi amigo el Che*, Editorial Sudamericana, Buenos Aires, 1996.

Saucedo Parada, Arnaldo, *No disparen... Soy el Che*, Editorial Oriente, Santa Cruz de la Sierra, 1986.

Taibo II, Paco Ignacio, *Guevara, Also Known as Che*, Planeta, Buenos Aires, 1997.

Villegas, Harry, *Pombo: A Man of Che's Guerrilla: With Che Guevara in Bolivia, 1966-1968*, Editora Política, Havana, 1996.

Other material on Ernesto "Che" Guevara

This includes many articles and speeches, compilations and excerpts. There are also various editions of his complete works.

Guevara, Ernesto Che, *Writings*, 1957-1967, Casa de las Américas, Havana, 1977.

- *Complete Works*, Legasa, Buenos Aires, 1997.

Writing:

- "Episodes from the revolutionary war"
- "Guerrilla Warfare"
- "Guerrilla Strategy and Tactics"
- "Socialism and the man in Cuba"
- "Create two, three... many Vietnams"

Diaries:

Ernesto "Che" Guevara kept diaries throughout his life; they contain some of his best pieces. Several have been recently edited like *Notas de viaje*. Of the others we know only a few fragments, for example as with his notes on the guerilla war in Africa; others remain unedited even today.

Guevara, Ernesto "Che", *Notas de viaje*, Centro Latinoamericano Che Guevara, Havana, 1993.

par Alvarez Tabío, Pedro, *War Diary: December 1956-February 1957*, Oficina de Publicaciones del Consejo de Estado, Havana, 1986.

Taibo II, Paco I.; Escobar, Froilán y Guerra, Félix, *El año en que estuvimos en ninguna parte*, Editorial Colihue, Buenos Aires, 1994.

The Bolivian Diary of Ernesto Che Guevara: November 7 1966, to October 7, 1967, Instituto del Libro, Havana, 1968.

Che's Bolivian Dairy (pictures and notes from the investigation by Adys Cupull and Froilán González], Editora Política, Havana, 1988.

CREDITS

PHOTO CREDITS
Abascal, Pedro: 211a
Alborta, Fredy: 188a, 190a, 191b, 192b, 193a, 195a
Andrew St. George: 66a
Andrew St. George/Magnum: 210-211
Courtesy of Carlos Barrios Barón Archive: 10c, 11a, 23a.
Clarín Archive: 181b
Clarín Archive /Fernando Dvoskin: 203f, 217
Corbalán Archive: 196a
Courtesy of Córdova Iturburu Archive: 18a, 18b, 21b
Courtesy of the Archive of the Faculty of Arts and Letters of the University of Havana: 201b Guevara Lynch Archive: 10a, 10b, 12a, 12b, 14a,16b, 17a, 19b, 20a, 20b, 22a, 23b, 24a, 25a, 26a, 26b, 27a, 28a, 28b, 28c, 29a, 29b, 30a, 31a, 33a, 48a, 50b, 51a, 56a
Courtesy of Hugo Gambini Archive: 141a
Liborio Noval Archive: 137a
Arnaldo Santos: 134a, 142b
Associated Press: 132a, 192b
Bildarchiv FotoMarburg: 189a, 195b
Billhardt, Thomas: 176b, 176d
Breccia, A./Oesterheld, H: 60c
BrunoBarbey/Magnum: 207b
Courtesy of Casa de las Américas: 46b, 46c, 49a, 49c, 49d, 107b, 118-119 bis, 121b, 166, 212b
Courtesy of Cerdini, Pablo: 212a
Chinolope: 126a
Corrales, Raúl: 105b, 109a, 109b, 127b, 128a, 128c, 129c, 206a
De Armas, Jorge: 203e
Dell'Orto, Gerardo: 213a, 213b
All rights reserved: 13a, 36a, 36-37, 39a, 57a, 57b, 57c, 57d, 78a, 98a, 118a, 142a, 144-145, 144a, 157a, 160a, 161, 165, 187c, 191a, 208b
Deutsche PresseAgentur: 150b, 151b
Courtesy of Austral newspaper (Temuco, Chile): 34a
Courtesy of Presencia newspaper: 41b
Courtesy of Dindo, Richard: 170a, 171a, 174a, 174b, 175a, 175b, 177a, 177b, 178b, 179a,180a.
Ediciones VerdeOlivo: 42a, 42b, 44a, 50a, 61b, 62b, 68a, 70a, 72a, 72b, 73b, 84b, 95a,96b, 98b, 100a, 101a, 104a, 116c, 122c, 125c, 128b, 131b, 139a, 146b, 147a,162c, 164b, 170b, 202b, 204a, 204b
Editora Política: 9b, 21a, 34b, 66b, 74b, 93a, 96a, 97a, 127c, 104b,119c, 141b, 145a, 146a, 160b, 162a, 162b, 163a, 167a, 173a, 182-183, 184a,184b, 194b, 219a
Editorial Capitán San Luis: 11b, 9a, 11c, 16a, 38b, 40b, 41a, 43a, 49b, 75b, 94a, 110b, 159b, 163c
Eisermann, Dirk: 209a
Faivre, Luis: 92a, 108a
Courtesy of Saucedo family: 178a, 180b, 181a, 182a, 183a, 186a, 186b, 187a
Figueroa, José A.: 58a, 203b, 203d
France Press: 172b, 173b
Courtesy of Foundation for Nature and Mankind: 71b, 77a, 80a, 80b, 81a, 82a, 82b, 83b, 87a, 87c, 94b, 140a, 201a

Holst, Jens: 214a
Klemm, Bárbara: 200a
Korda, Alberto: front cover, 93b, 95b, 102a, 102b, 110c, 122a, 122b, 134b, 134c, 136c, 138a, 143a, 154b, 197a, 198a, 198-199
Lee Lockwood/Das Fotoarchiv: 45b, 139b, 203a, 205b
Courtesy of Longoni, Eduardo: 35b, 40a, 168-169
Mauritshuis, LaHaya: 194a
Noval, Liborio: 6-7, 115b, 130-131
Office for Historical Affairs: 8a, 13b, 15a, 17b, 19a, 31b, 32a, 33b, 34c, 35a, 38a, 44b,46a, 47a, 51b, 52a, 53a, 53b, 54a, 55a, 55b, 56b, 57e, 59a, 59b, 61a, 62a, 63a, 64a, 64b, 67a, 68b, 69a, 70b, 71a, 73a, 74a, 75a, 76b, 78-79, 82-83, 84a, 85a, 86a, 88a, 90a, 90b, 100b, 101b, 106b, 107a, 110a, 126b, 133b, 135b, 148a, 151a, 158a, 159a
Oller, Jorge: 145b
Courtesy of Liliana Porter: 218a
Prensa Latina: 106a, 120a, 124a, 124b, 125a, 125b, 127a, 131a, 136a, 136b, 150a, 152b,153a, 153b, 154a, 169a, 172a, 176a, 176c, 176e, 185b, 187b, 208a, 209b
Ramparts: 207a
Reuter: 216c
Bohemia magazine: 65a, 76a, 79a, 97b, 99b, 105a, 107c, 110-111, 114b, 119d, 123a,123b, 132b, 133a, 135a, 148-149, 152a, 153c, 156a, 164a, 183b, 185a, 190b, 196b, 200b
Romero, Prefecto: 60a, 60b, 83a, 87b, 88b, 89a, 91a, 99a, 115a, 117a, 117b, 140b
Courtesy of Roque, Adalberto: 203c, 216a, 216b
Salas: 103a, 111a, 112-113, 114a, 116a, 116b,118-119, 121a, 155a, 163b, 214-215, back page.
Time Magazine: 112a
UPI/ Corbis Bettmann: 45a, 138b, 206b
Vander Hilst, Robert: 205a

The statements and excerpts that accompany the photographs have been taken from the following works:

Aguirre, Mirta, "Canción antigua al Che Guevara".
Anderson, Jon Lee, Che Guevara: A Revolutionary Life, © Grove Press, New York, 1997.
Báez, Luis, Secretos de generales, © Editorial Si-Mar, Havana, 1996.
Baudelaire, Charles, Le fleurs du mal, © Les editions G. Crès, Paris, 1930.
Berger, John, "The Legendary Che Guevara Is Dead", in New Society, New York, 1967.
Borges, Jorge Luis, Obras completas, © Emecé,Buenos Aires, 1974.
Breccia, Alberto; Breccia, Enrique y Oesterheld, Héctor, Che, © Ikusager,Vitoria-Gasteiz, 1987.
Cardenal,Ernesto, En Cuba, © Era, México DF, 1977.
Castañeda, Jorge, La vida en rojo, © Planeta, Buenos Aires, 1997.
Castro, Fidel, La historia me absolverá, © Oficina de Publicaciones del Consejo de Estado, Havana, 1993.
Castro, Fidel, "Speech delivered in the Plaza de la Revolution, at the Commemoration Service for Che", special edition of Bohemia magazine,

Havana, 1967.
Castro, Fidel, "Llamado a los intelectuales".
Castro, Fidel, "Speech delivered at the opening session of the Central Committee of the Cuban Communist Party", © Bohemia magazine, 8 December 1965.
Cortázar, Julio, Ultimoround, © Siglo XXI, México DF, 1969.
Cupull, Adys andGonzález, Froilán, Cálida presencia, © Oriente, Santiago de Cuba, 1995.
– De Ñacahuazú a La Higuera, © Editora Política, Havana, 1994.
Debray, Régis, Les Masques, © Gallimard, Paris, 1987.
Franqui, Carlos, Cuba, el libro de los 12, © Era, México DF, 1966.
Felipe, León, Antología rota, © Losada, Buenos Aires, 1972.
Gadea, Hilda, Años decisivos, © Aguilar, México DF, 1972.
García Marruz, Fina, Visitaciones, © Ediciones Unión, Havana, 1970.
Guevara, Ernesto Che, Obras, 1957-1967, © Casa de las Américas, Havana, 1977.
– Obras completas, © Legasa, Buenos Aires, 1997.
Guevara Lynch,Ernesto, Mi hijo el Che, © Planeta, Barcelona, 1981
– Aquí va un soldado de América, © Sudamericana/Planeta, Buenos Aires, 1987.
Guevara de la Serna, Ernesto, Notas de viaje, © Centro Latinoamericano Che Guevara, Havana, 1993.
Ginsberg, Allen, "Elegy for Che Guevara" en La caída de América, © Visor, Madrid, 1980.
Korol, Claudia, El Che y los argentinos, © Ediciones Dialéctica, Buenos Aires,1988.
Lezama Lima, José, "Ernesto Guevara, comandante nuestro", en Casa de las Américas, Havana, January/February, 1968.
Ludwig, Emil, Goethe, Geschichte eines Menschen, © C. Bertelsmann Verlag, 1959.
Masetti, Jorge R., Los que luchan y losque lloran, © Edición cubana, Havana, 1960.
Massari, Roberto, Che Guevara, grandeza y riesgo de lautopía, © Txalaparta, Tafala, 1993.
Mercado, Tununa, "El Diario de Bolivia", en Casa de las Américas, January/March, 1997.
Neruda, Pablo, "Farewell", en Crepusculario, © Editorial Andrés Bello, Santiago de Chile, 1995.
Orozco, Olga, "No hay puertas" en Antología © Editorial Corregidor, Buenos Aires, 1989.
Rodríguez, ReinaMaría, "Un simple clic del disparador", poema inédito,1997.
Subcomandante Marcos, "Discurso de cierre en el Encuentro Intercontinental por la humanidad y contra el neoliberalismo" en LaJornada, México DF, 4 April 1997.
Taibo II, Paco Ignacio, Ernesto Guevara, también conocidocomo el Che, © Planeta, Buenos Aires, 1997.
Revista Time, 8 August 1960.
Urondo, Francisco, "Descarga", en Casa de las Américas, Havana, January/February, 1968.
Vallejo, César, Los heraldos negros, © Losada, Buenos Aires, 1961.